CHRISTMAS WRAPPED IN LOVE

CHRISTMAS WRAPPED IN LOVE

Alice Joyce Davidson

ABINGDON PRESS

Nashville

CHRISTMAS WRAPPED IN LOVE

Copyright © 1987 by Abingdon Press

All rights reserved.
No part of this work may be reproduced or transmitted in any form or by any means, electronic or mechanical, including photocopying and recording, or by any information storage or retrieval system, except as may be expressly permitted by the 1976 Copyright Act or in writing from the publisher. Requests for permission should be addressed in writing to Abingdon Press, 201 Eighth Avenue South, Nashville, TN 37202.

This book is printed on acid-free paper.

Library of Congress Cataloging-in-Publication Data

DAVIDSON, ALICE JOYCE.
  Christmas wrapped in love.
  1. Christmas. 2. Christmas cookery. 3. Christmas decorations. I. Title
     GT4985.D44   1987   394.2'68282   87-11510

ISBN 0-687-07818-0

Manufactured by the Parthenon Press at
Nashville, Tennessee, United States of America

For Marvin

*A special thank you to Carol Kessler
for her help with the recipes,
and to Jerry F. for his help through the years.*

Contents

PART 1: THE FEELINGS OF CHRISTMAS

WRAPPED WITH LOVE—13

Joy to the World—13 God's Gift to All—14 As the Christmas Bells Chime—15 Finding Christmas—16 To a Dear Friend—17 A Child Is Born—18 The First Time and the Last—19 Memories of Christmas—20 A Christmas Recipe—20 Grandma's Early Start—21 Peace on Earth—22 A Christmas Blessing—23 Thank You Prayer—23 The Churchbells—24 Wishes—24 Living Christmas All Year—25 Keeping the Glow—26 Christmas Is Love—28 Christmas Twinkle—29 God's Son Is Born—29 Christmas Blessing for a Home—30 A Grace—30 A Christmas Prayer—31 A New Year's Prayer for Peace—32

FOR THE YOUNG AND YOUNG AT HEART—33

A Gift of Love—35

CHRISTMAS FAVORITES—49

from Little Town of Bethlehem—49 from Hark, the Glad Sound—49 from Christmas—50 from In the Bleak Midwinter—50 from Shepherds, Rejoice—50 from Christmas—51 from At the Sign of the Jolly Jack—51 from Holly Song (from As You Like It)—51 Yes, Virginia,

There Is a Santa Claus!—52 A Visit from St. Nicholas—54 The Mahogany Tree—56 Peace on Earth—58 A Lullaby for Christmas—60 Cradle Hymn—61 Hark! the Herald Angels—62 The Shepherds Had an Angel—64

PART 2: LOVE FROM THE KITCHEN

APPETIZERS AND SOUPS—69

Cheese Trees—69 Onion Soup au Gratin—69 Vegy-Cheese Soup—70 Lentil Soup—70 Clam Chowder—71 Chicken Liver Pâté—71 Spinach-Onion Dip—72 Curry Dip—72 Cucumber and Dill Dip—72 Stuffed Cherry Tomatoes—72

ENTRÉES—73

Baked Ham with Dijon Sauce—73 Scalloped Ham and Potatoes—73 Turkey Roast Supreme—74 Turkey Tetrazzini—74 Curried Turkey Salad—75 Turkey Meatballs with Sweet and Sour Sauce—75 Shepherd's Pie—76 Deep Dish Lamb Stew—76 Italian Swiss Steak—77 Frosted Meat Loaf—77 Stroganoff Meatballs—77 Ham and Cheese Quiche—78 Hearty Meatballs and Cabbage—78 Barbecued Pot Roast—79 Zesty Chicken Breasts—79 Ginger Chicken Salad—79

SALADS AND SIDE DISHES—80

Vegetables au Gratin—80 Glazed Carrots—80 Cheese Potato Balls—81 Walnut Candied Sweet Potatoes—81 Scalloped Spinach and Pimiento—81 Grandma's Red Cabbage—82 Wax Beans and Bacon—82 Red and Green Coleslaw—82 Tomato Aspic—83 Marinated Snow Peas and Carrots—83 Creamy Hot Potato Salad—83 Frozen Cranberry-Orange Salad—84 Spinach and Lettuce Salad—84 Five Bean Salad—85 Christmas Antipasto—85 Holiday Waldorf Salad—86 Honey-Cream Fruit Bowl—86 Double Corn Fritters—87 Corn Pudding—87 Apple-Raisin-Rice Pudding—87 Apricot Noodle Pudding—88 Wheat and Raisin Stuffing—88

BREADS—89

Cheese Party Rye—89 Cranberry Muffins—89 Oatmeal Rolls—90 Banana Bread—90 Onion Hot Bread—91 Zucchini Fruit Bread—91 Pumpkin-Nut Bread—91 Applesauce Pancakes—92

BEVERAGES—93

Orange-Nog—93 Eggnog—93 Cran-Orange Julius—94 Lemon-Orange Punch—94 Honey Apple Tea—94 Cran-Apple Refresher—95 Kiddie Kooler—95 Spiced Tomato Juice—95 Cocoa Coffee—95 Hot Apple Cider—96 Fruited Ice Mold—96

COOKIES, DESSERTS, CANDY—97

Spritz Cookies—97 Danish Butter Cookies—97 Peanut Butter Wreaths—98 Gingerbread Cookies—98 Double Chocolate Chip Cookies—99 Macaroons—99 Cloud Cookies—100 Lacy Oat Cookies—100 Pecan Drop Cookies—101 Filbert Snow Balls—101 Milk Chocolate Walnut Bars—102 Raspberry Bars—102 Date and Orange Bars—103 Holiday Honey-Fruit Bars—103 Chewy Saucepan Brownies—104 Saucepan Blondies—104 Chocolate Meringues—105 Strawberry Coconut Meringues—105 Apple Crisp—105 Plums and Pudding—106 Frozen Lime Pie—106 Poppy Seed Slices—107 Mixed Nut Pralines—107 White Raisin Clusters—107 Honey Nuts—108 Uncooked Fondant—108 Fondant Stuffed Dates—109 Double Peanut Brittle—109 English Toffee—109 Fruit and Nut Balls—110

PART 3: THE HOUSEHOLD WRAPPED IN LOVE

CRAFTS—*113*

Gift Wrapping Ideas—113 Salt-and-Flour Clay—114 Pom Pom Decorations—115 Stained-"Glass" Ornaments—116 Foil Gift-Wrap Decorations—118 Clothespin Dolls—119 Foil Pan Ornaments—120 Finger Puppets—121 Tissue Paper Poinsettias—122 Sachets—123 Stuffed Felt Ornaments—124 Patterns—124

PART 1
The Feelings of Christmas

Every spiritual bouquet
Sent from God above
Was custom picked for each of us,
Then wrapped and tied with love!

WRAPPED WITH LOVE

Joy to the World

It's joy
   and good cheer time,
It's memories
   are near time,
It's all
   we hold dear time—
IT'S CHRISTMAS!

. . . I bring you good tidings of great joy, which shall be to all people. For unto you is born this day in the city of David a Saviour, which is Christ the Lord.

Luke 2:10, 11

God's Gift to All

God's gifts are plentiful and good.
We find them everywhere.
He gave us oceans filled with life,
Mountains carved with care,
Fluffy clouds in bright blue skies,
And birds that fill the air.

God's gifts are all around us.
He gave us things like these—
Rainbows after showers,
A cool refreshing breeze,
The sunshine, pretty flowers,
And sturdy shady trees.

God's gifts are truly splendid;
But when all is said and done,
His greatest gift—the gift of gifts
He gave to everyone
Is the one He gave at Christmas—
His only begotten Son!

As the Christmas Bells Chime

There's a Santa on each corner.
There's a big tree on the square,
And some good old-fashioned caroling
Has warmed the winter air.

Heigh ho! It's a merry old time.
The earth sings of love
   as the Christmas bells chime!

There's a baby asleep in the manager,
And the angels descend from above
Singing, "Glory to God in the Highest,"
And tell of the gift of His love.

Heigh ho! It's a glorious time.
The earth sings of love
   as the Christmas bells chime!

Finding Christmas

It's easy to find Christmas.
It permeates the air
With sights and sounds of happiness
For everyone to share.

But this happy, holy season
Encompasses much more
Than plastic decorations
Or a wreath upon a door.

We celebrate the Savior's birth,
A gift from God above
Who sent His only Son to earth
To fill the world with love!

To a Dear Friend

Dear Friend,

Christmas is nearing and it brings back so many memories. I remember when I first found *you* for a friend. I was just a little tyke feeling sad and lonely. Then I discovered *you* and my sadness and loneliness vanished.

Because of *you*, I discovered what a friend is. A friend is someone who shares your hopes, your dreams, and your plans. A friend helps light the way when it is dark, and helps chase away the clouds. And when a storm comes a friend is there to shelter you beneath an open umbrella. A friend is someone you can depend on. Whether you stay close or move away, you can call on a friend and count on a friend—always, anytime, and anyplace.

A friend is someone who encourages you to walk the right path, do what you should, and be the very best you can be.

Dear friend, I know that I may have drifted away from *you* at times; but that was only on the surface. *You* have always been and always will be a part of my life . . . a part of my heart. How can it be otherwise? *You* were with me when I lost a toy, lost a pet, and later lost a job . . . and lost my father. *You* were with me when I found love, found my husband, found myself with child, and found *myself*.

Christmas is nearing. That means *your* birthday is drawing close. I can never repay *you* on *your* birthday for all *you* have given me; but my *Dear Friend*, I give *you* my love. I give *you* myself.

Happy birthday, Jesus! And thank You for being my Friend!

THE FEELINGS OF CHRISTMAS ~ 17

A Child Is Born

Hush dear Baby
Don't You cry.
The manger keeps You
Warm and dry.

You've come to us
Of humble birth
To bring God's love
And peace to earth.

Hush dear Baby
Small and sweet,
You'll spread God's word
To all You meet.

The angels sing
With dulcet voices
As in Your birth
The earth rejoices!

The First Time and the Last

Blessed Baby
    Curled up in a manger
    roughly hewn of wood
    He lies
    Seeing for the first time
    His loving mother's eyes.

Blessed Savior
    Stretched upon a humble cross
    roughly hewn of wood
    He dies
    seeing for the last time
    His loving mother's eyes.

Memories of Christmas

Stringing popcorn, wrapping gifts,
Playing in the snow,
Hanging decorations,
The Christmas tree aglow,
Telling stories, singing songs,
Displaying family treasures—
Cherished family memories
Are made from childhood pleasures!

A Christmas Recipe

Give Christmas Day the proper start
By waking with a joy-filled heart,
Then fill your holiday with these:
Family, friends, and memories,
Add some laughter, songs to sing,
Gifts to open, gifts to bring;
Then to make it more delicious
Mix in dreams and new year wishes,
The sweetest kind of Christmas love,
And special blessings from above!

Grandma's Early Start

When the days began to shorten, when the air took on a crispness, when the first tint of yellow outlined a leaf, we knew it was time to visit Grandma.

Grandma lived only an hour away, but it seemed like hours and hours to me. A visit meant special activities, special food, and lots of loving attention. Located at the edge of the city, her big white frame house was surrounded by a huge yard covered "wall to wall" with fruit trees. Crab apples, pears, peaches, plums grew in abundance there. A great big apple tree up against the far side of the fence acted as host to a group of grape vines hanging heavy with purple clusters. We'd come at "picking time" to gather in the harvest. I helped pick grapes and collected fruit from the lower branches and the ground; but my favorite job was helping Grandma in the kitchen. I especially enjoyed pitting plums. When a little pulp would stick, I'd chew it off then suck the pits, storing them squirrel-like till my cheeks would almost burst.

Watching Grandma bake fascinated me. She never measured—a handful of this, a pinch of that, a couple of eggs; and she'd beat, beat, beat the dough with a big wooden spoon while her generous form rippled from the action. I remember the smell of sweet spices mingling with fruit juices as a plum cake baked; and I can still taste that first warm, moist bite. Yum! My favorite treat was Grandma's plum preserves. I'd get to help make that. Using instinct Grandma would cover a mound of plums with just the right amount of sugar. As the sugar dissolved over a low flame, I'd use a big wooden spoon and stir until the juice became transparent; then Grandma would take over and give the mixture a quick boil so the plums wouldn't fall apart. She portioned the candied-like fruit into canning jars, putting aside a small one for us to take home along with baskets of crab apples, pears, and grapes. When Christmas came the family would be treated to decorated jars filled with preserves, jams, and relishes.

It's been a long time since I went to Grandma's. I was only nine when she passed away; but when "picking time" comes and I begin to make my Christmas treats from the bounty in my yard, memory takes me back to Grandma's kitchen once again.

Peace on Earth

Oh, Prince of Peace, You came to earth
So many, many years ago
To bring God's love and spread good will
To all who dwell on earth below.

We learn about the words you preached
In every church and Sunday school,
And, yes, we even know by heart
Your very precious Golden Rule.

But we're too caught up in ourselves
To put in practice what we learn.
Peace is still a dream to us,
And year to year a grave concern.

Oh, Prince of Peace, we bow our heads
This day we celebrate Your birth,
And pray Your gospel from above
Of brotherhood, good will, and love
Will bring the peace we're dreaming of
To all who dwell upon this earth.

A Christmas Blessing

May Christmas
light a torch
in your heart
that glows with
the warmest of lights . . .

And may that glow
bring joy to you
and brighten
the darkest of nights!

Thank You Prayer

With happy hearts
  we say a prayer
To thank You, Father
  for your care
And all Your loving gifts
  we share
    at Christmas!

We thank You for
  good will, good cheer,
For having friends
  and family near
For giving us
  our Savior dear
    at Christmas!

THE FEELINGS OF CHRISTMAS ~ 23

The Churchbells

It's Christmastime, it's Christmastime!
The strong sweet notes of churchbells chime.
And with each ring
The churchbells sing,
"Christ the Lord was born today!"

Sing a song of joy and mirth
For Christ was sent to walk on earth
And bring God's love
Down from above—
"Christ the Lord was born today!"

The sounds of Christmas fill the air.
They ring out, sing out everywhere,
For Christmas is a time of cheer,
A blessed holy time of year—
"Christ the Lord was born today!"

Wishes

What are you wishing for, dear little boy
The night that Santa Claus comes?
   A computer, a robot, a space station, too,
   And a bugle and very loud drums!

What are you wishing for, sweet little girl,
What are you wishing for, Dear?
   A spaceship, computer, a robot, some drums,
   And a bugle that plays loud and clear!

Living Christmas All Year

On Christmas Day and always, too,
God sends his love to me and you.
He sends His blessings day by day
To all who walk within His way.

Now wouldn't it be lovely, too,
If we gave heartgifts all year through?
For every day's a special day
To send a heartgift on its way!

Keeping the Glow

The spirit of Christmas is wonderful! It seeps into our lives making everything we do take on a loving glow. Wouldn't it be wonderful if we could capture that spirit all year? Here are **101** ways to keep the spirit of Christmas glowing till Christmas comes again:

1. Smile at a stranger. **2.** Smile at a friend. **3.** Smile at a baby. **4.** Babysit. **5.** Share a recipe. **6.** Share a joke. **7.** Share a memory. **8.** Share a happy moment. **9.** Share a sunset. **10.** Share someone's grief. **11.** Share some spare time. **12.** Share a double-fudge brownie. **13.** Give a compliment. **14.** Visit the sick. **15.** Visit the elderly. **16.** Take someone shopping. **17.** Do someone's shopping. **18.** Carry someone's groceries. **19.** Do someone's laundry. **20.** Mow someone's lawn. **21.** Pull someone's weeds. **22.** Read to a child. **23.** Read to an elderly person. **24.** Write a thank-you note. **25.** Write a love note. **26.** Right a wrong. **27.** Volunteer at church. **28.** Volunteer at school. **29.** Volunteer for your community. **30.** Phone a friend. **31.** Phone someone you love. **32.** Phone a shut-in. **33.** Sew on a button for someone. **34.** Bake a cake for someone. **35.** Be honest with your praise. **36.** Be honest with your loved ones. **37.** Be honest with your finances. **38.** Help someone wash a car. **39.** Give someone a lift in your car. **40.** Lift someone's spirits. **41.** Be patient. **42.** Be considerate.

26 ~ *CHRISTMAS WRAPPED IN LOVE*

43. Be understanding. **44.** Be on time. **45.** Be nice to loved ones. **46.** Be nice to strangers. **47.** Be nice to friends. **48.** Make a new friend. **49.** Make someone proud of you. **50.** Make someone feel proud. **51.** Make someone feel loved. **52.** Make someone feel needed. **53.** Make a big pot of chili. **54.** Honor your parents. **55.** Honor your children. **56.** Act honorable. **57.** Be a good neighbor. **58.** Be a good relative. **59.** Be a good friend. **60.** Be a good citizen. **61.** Be a good sport. **62.** Help someone do better. **63.** Help someone think better. **64.** Help someone feel better. **65.** Help someone grow. **66.** Grow closer to a loved one. **67.** Grow a garden. **68.** Be kind to a pet. **69.** Be kind to your neighbor's pet. **70.** Be kind to your neighbor's children. **71.** Remember birthdays. **72.** Remember anniversaries. **73.** Remember special occasions. **74.** Give gifts graciously. **75.** Receive gifts graciously. **76.** Do no evil. **77.** Hear no evil. **78.** See no evil. **79.** Fight evil. **80.** Fight pollution. **81.** Work for peace. **82.** Work hard. **83.** Work with a smile. **84.** Be loving. **85.** Be lovable. **86.** Love the unlovable. **87.** Be true to your friends. **88.** Be true to your neighbors. **89.** Be true to your family. **90.** Be true to yourself. **91.** Be open-minded. **92.** Be open-handed. **93.** Lend a book. **94.** Lend a hand. **95.** Lend an ear. **96.** Lend a cup of sugar. **97.** Pray for your family. **98.** Pray for your friends. **99.** Pray for yourself. **100.** Thank God for His gifts. **101.** Keep Jesus alive in your heart.

Christmas Is Love

Christmas is love,
And love is a gift—
A wonderful feeling
That gives life a lift.

Christmas is love,
And love is a power
That's strong and yet sweet
As a delicate flower.

Christmas is love,
And love is a light—
A comforting candle
That glows in the night.

Christmas is love,
And love is the force
That can set all the world
On a more peaceful course.

Christmas is love,
And love's the reward
We get from believing
In Christ, our dear Lord!

Christmas Twinkle

Lord, put a smile on my lips,
A twinkle in my eye
So I can give a bit of cheer
To all whom I pass by!

Lord, put compassion in my heart,
And give me warmth, I pray,
So I can pass a bit of love
To all who come my way!

God's Son Is Born

Who came to earth to free us all
From shame, from sin, from strife?
Who brought the sacred promise
Of an everlasting life?

Your Son, Your Son, Your only Son
Who shared Your love with everyone!

Who spread Your gospel everywhere
To all who came His way?
Who took a cross upon His back
And died for us one day?

Your Son, Your Son, Your only Son,—
Oh, God on high, Your will be done!

THE FEELINGS OF CHRISTMAS ~ 29

Christmas Blessing for a Home

Lord, bless this home this Christmas season.
Let it be a haven for
Those who live here, relatives,
And friends who enter through the door.

Lord, bless this home this Christmas season.
Fill each room from wall to wall
With Christmas cheer and joy and laughter,
And love within us one and all.

Lord, bless this home this Christmas season.
Let it be a place to share
All the loving gifts You've given,
Songs of praise, and earnest prayer.

A Grace

We sit around the table
And we bow our heads in prayer
To thank You, loving Father,
For Your guidance and Your care.

May this food we take together
On this Christmas Holiday
Refresh us and sustain us
As we follow in Your way.

May the food from all Your teachings
Fill our hearts and minds and souls
And give us strength and courage
To reach for higher goals!

A Christmas Prayer

Dear God,

Let my vision widen
To the glory of Your ways.
Fill my lips with gospel
And joyous words of praise.

Use my mind and fill it full
Of righteous goals and deeds.
Give my hands some noble work
To help fill others' needs.

Take my soul, take all of me
And make me worth of
Your priceless gift of Christmas—
Your treasured gift of love!

A New Year's Prayer for Peace

Dear Lord,

Let this be a year
that moves us
one step closer
to each other.

Let this be a year
that brings us
understanding in our hearts.

Let this be a year
that fills us
with a yearning
burning feeling
for peace with one another
and a oneness, Lord, with You!

FOR THE YOUNG
AND YOUNG AT HEART

Christmas is a time of joy
For every little girl and boy—
A time of celebration when
All hearts are light . . . and young again!

A Gift of Love

Christmastime in Toyland
Was just two days away,
And all of Santa's helpers
Were preparing for that day.

They dusted and they polished.
They cleaned and waxed the floor.
Then most of them went shopping
At the special Christmas store.

Every little helper
Competed with the rest
To buy the Christmas present
Santa Claus would choose as best.

But one good helper, Charity,
Had nothing she could spend,
For she lent all her savings
To help a needy friend.

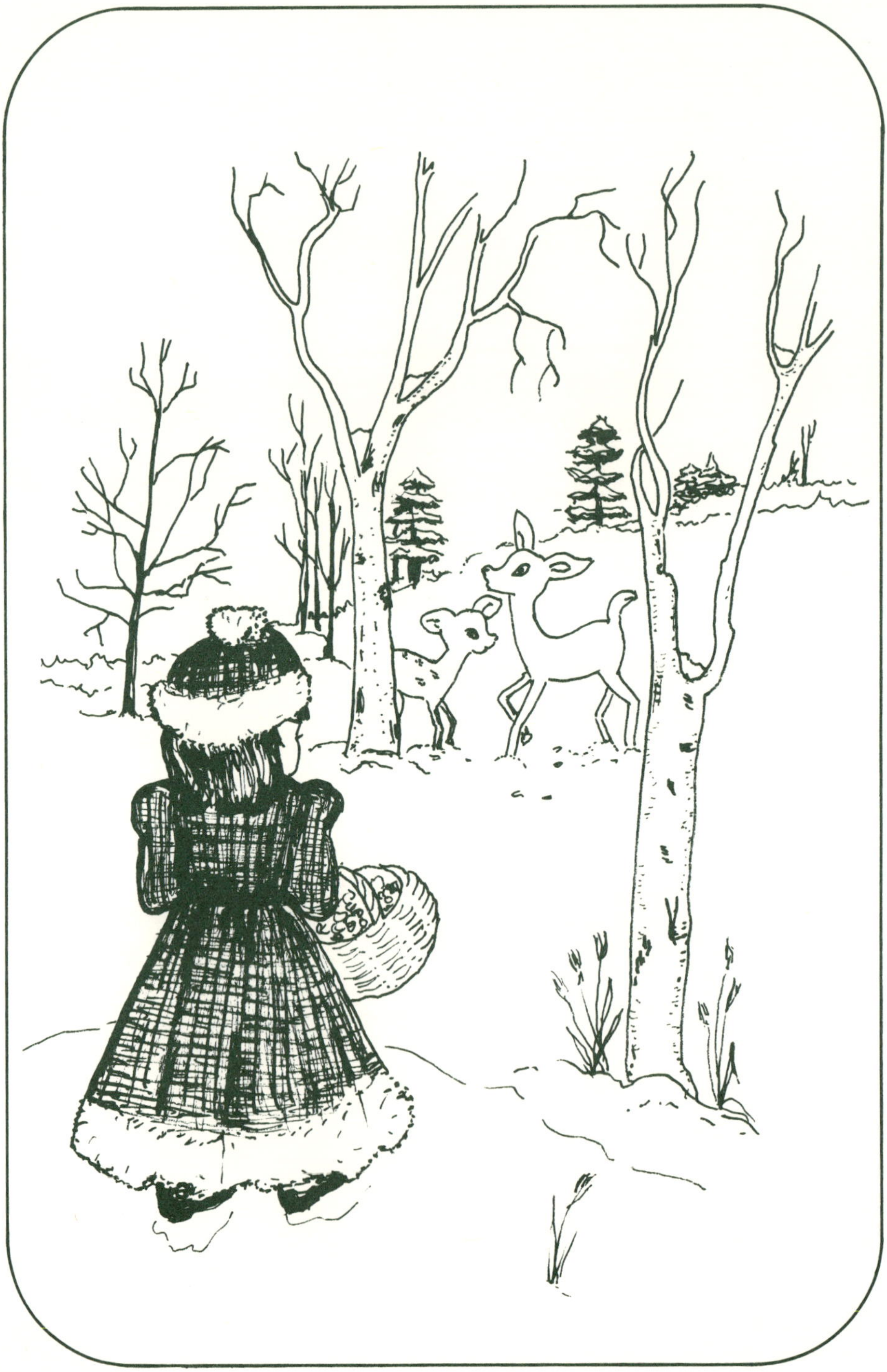

Thought Charity, "I'll make a gift—
Something good to eat.
I'll bake a lovely nut cake
For Santa's Christmas treat."

Then off she went to gather nuts,
And in the woods she found
Some pine nuts, which were hidden in
The soft snow on the ground.

As Charity went home again
She almost stumbled on
A lovely doe, and cuddled near
A precious little fawn.

They both looked very hungry,
So Charity was glad
To give them all the pine nuts,
Everything she had.

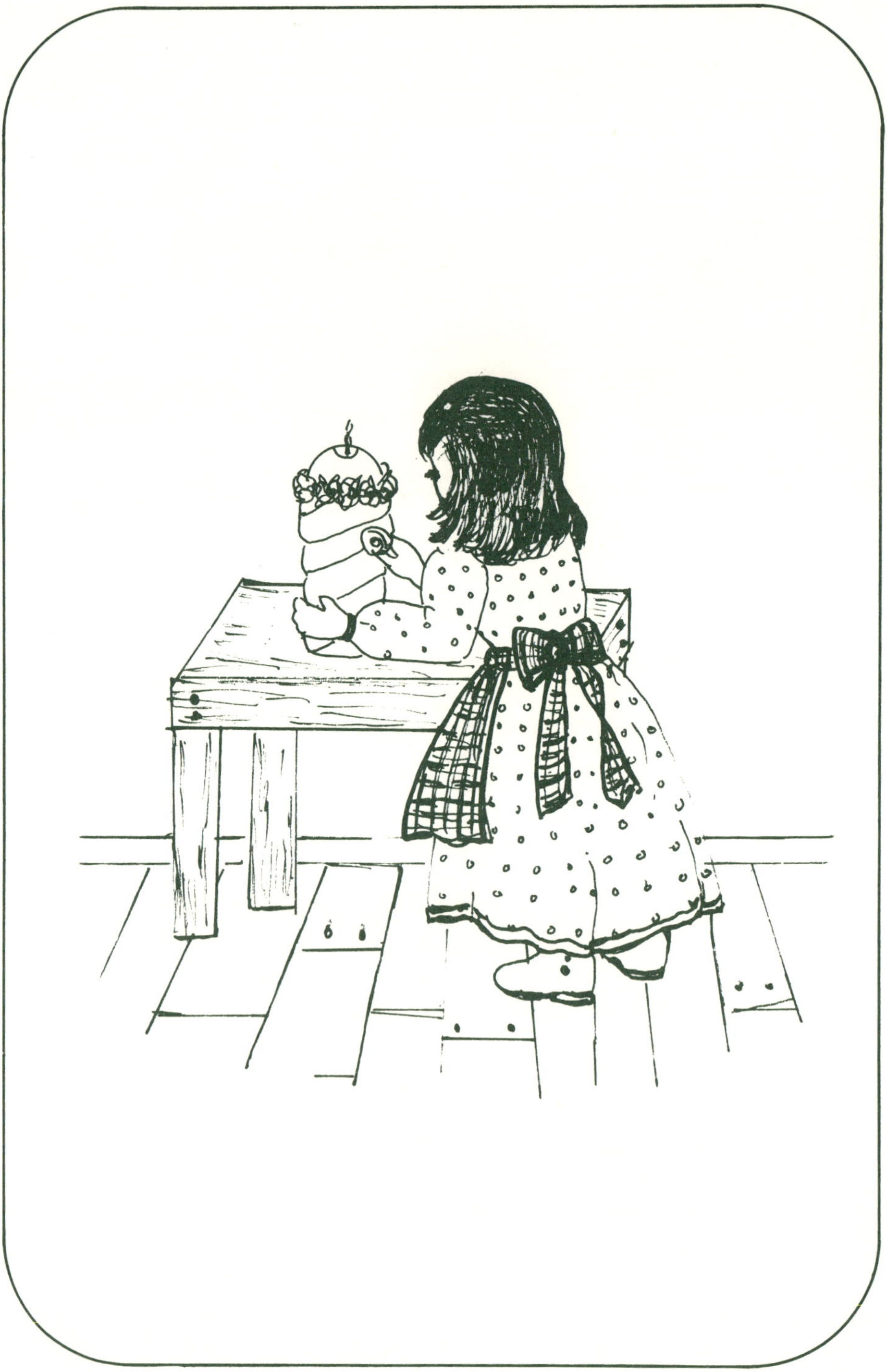

"Though I can't bake a nut cake
For Santa's gift," she said,
"I'll make a different present
When tomorrow comes instead."

The next day came and Charity
Began another gift—
A homemade Christmas candle
To give Santa's heart a lift.

She dipped a wick in melted wax
And worked for many hours
Adding swirls and lovely curls
Entwined with leaves and flowers.

To make sure that the candle burnt
She lit the twisted wick,
Then Charity heard someone call,
"Help! Please hurry! Quick!"

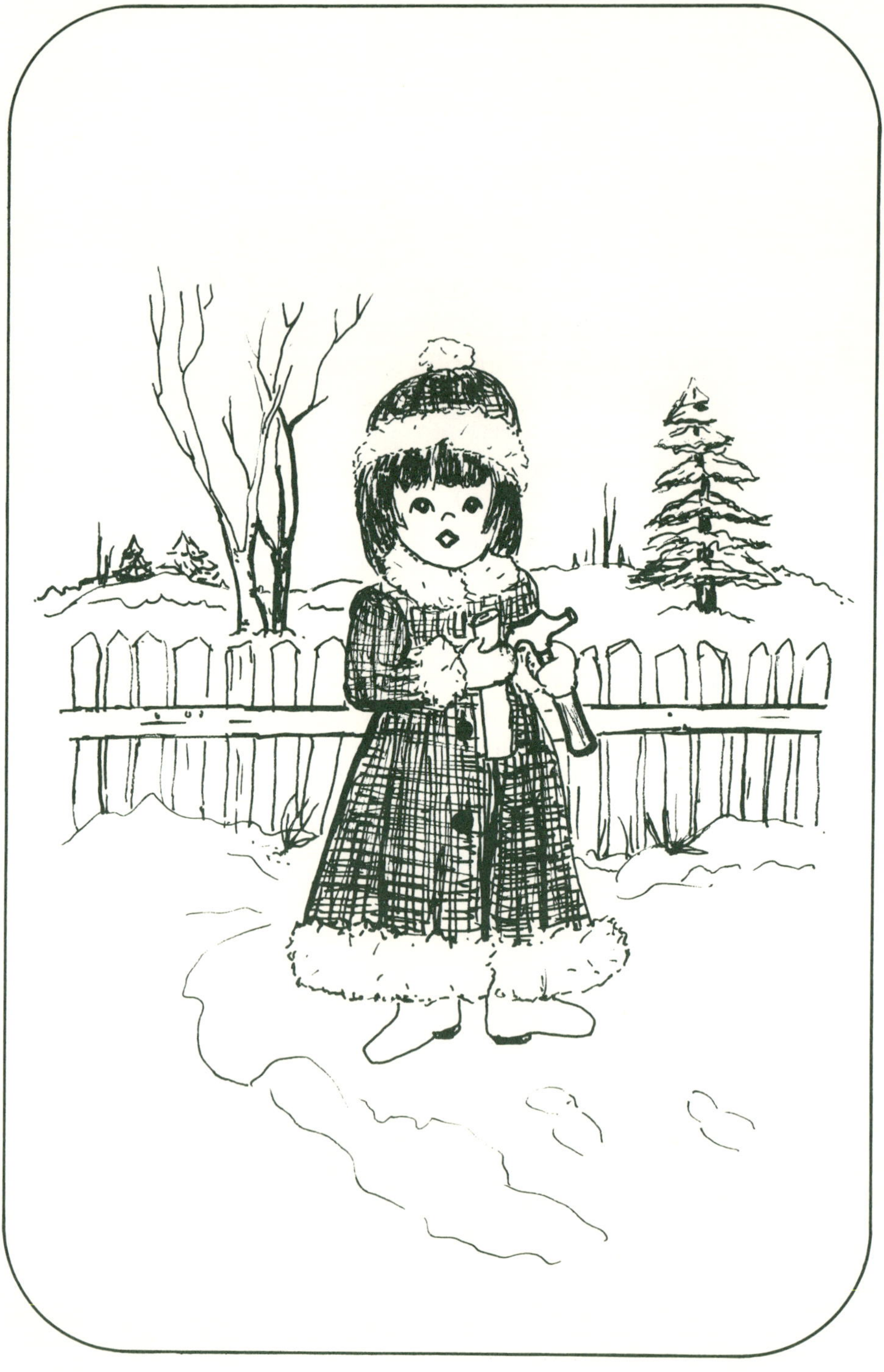

She was so very worried
When she heard that frantic shout,
She rushed outside and didn't blow
Her lovely candle out.

Next door she saw her neighbor
Who was stuck high in a tree.
"My ladder fell and broke," he sighed.
"Please try to rescue me."

Charity got scraps of wood,
Some nails, a hammer, too,
And fixed her neighbor's ladder
Till it was good as new.

When he was safe, she went back home.
She opened up her door
To see her lovely candle
Had melted on the floor.

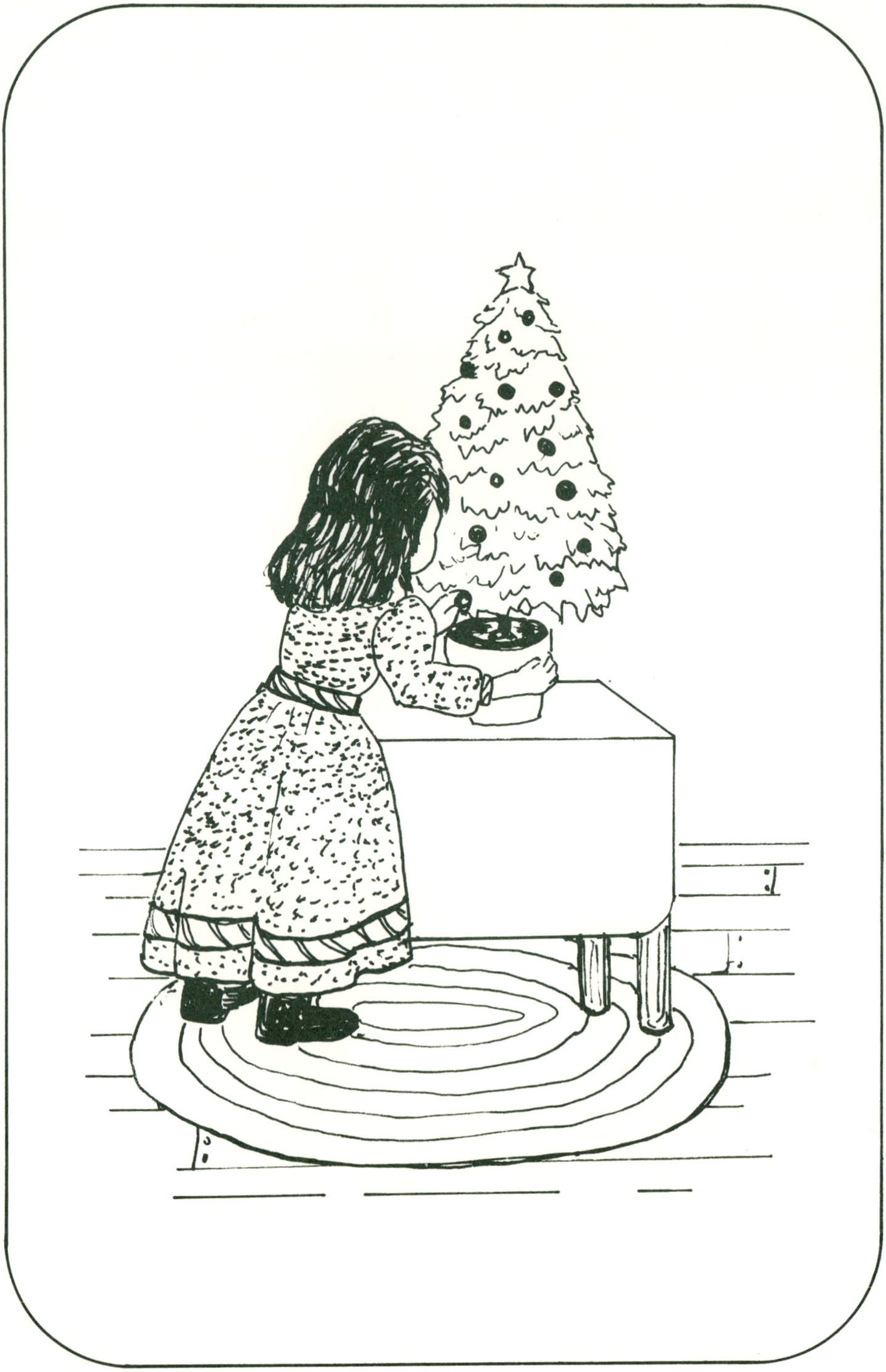

"Now I don't have a candle
For Santa's gift," she said.
"I'll have to think of something new
When morning comes instead."

Then next day came and Charity
Thought, "Christmas Day is here.
Santa's party is today,
And I've no gift, I fear."

"I'll take a trip into the woods
And find a little tree
Then decorate it as a gift
For Santa Claus from me."

She brought a little tree back home.
She trimmed it with bright bows,
Then baked some ginger cookies
To fill between the rows.

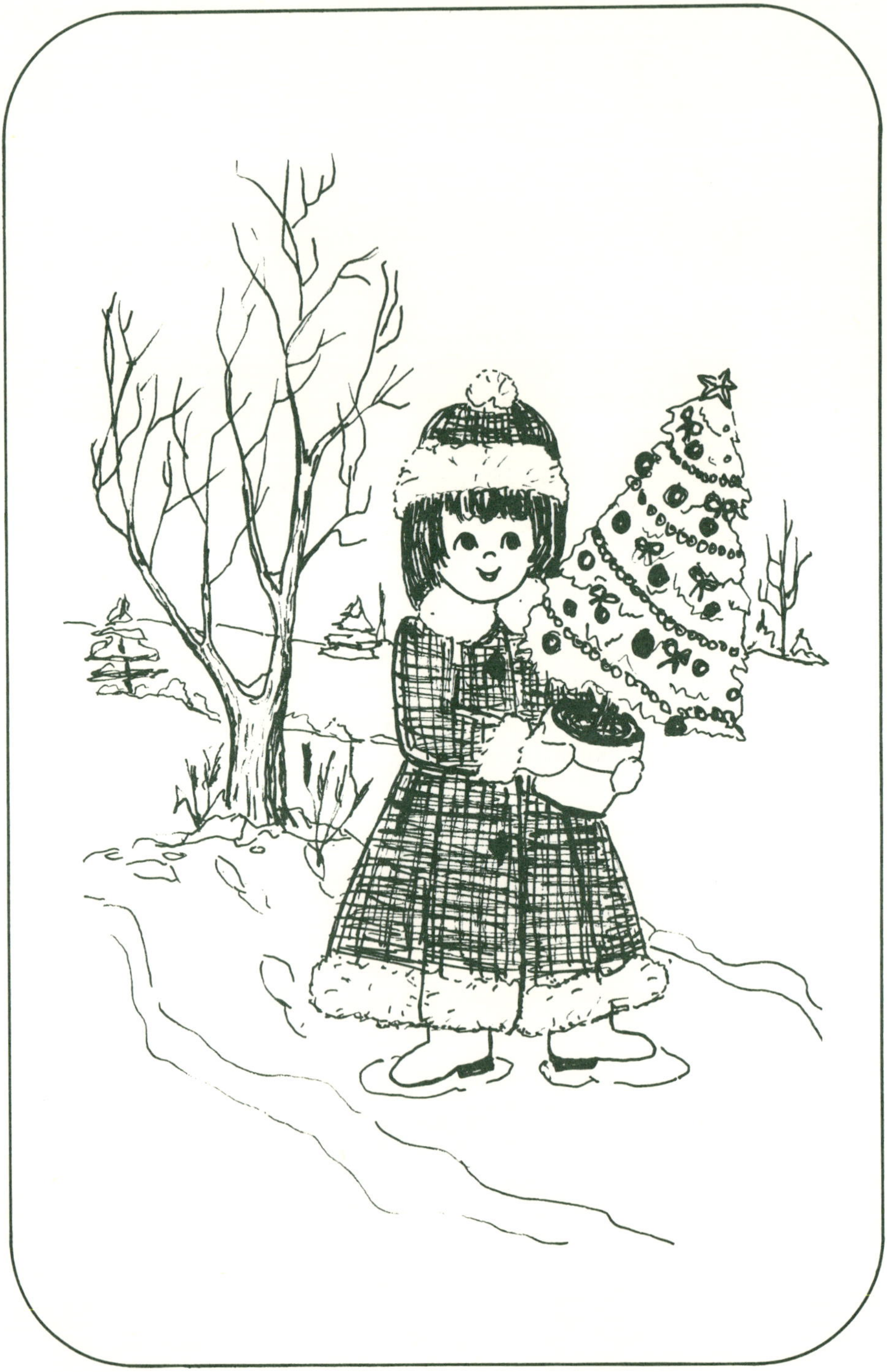

The little tree was beautiful,
And Charity was glad;
But on the way to Santa's home
She came upon a lad.

His eyes were filled with teardrops.
He was sad as he could be,
For his family was too poor to buy
The smallest Christmas tree.

So Charity gave him the tree.
She sighed, and then said,
"I guess I'll think of something new
For Santa's gift instead."

At Santa's house each helper
Had competed with the rest
To buy the special present
That dear Santa would like best.

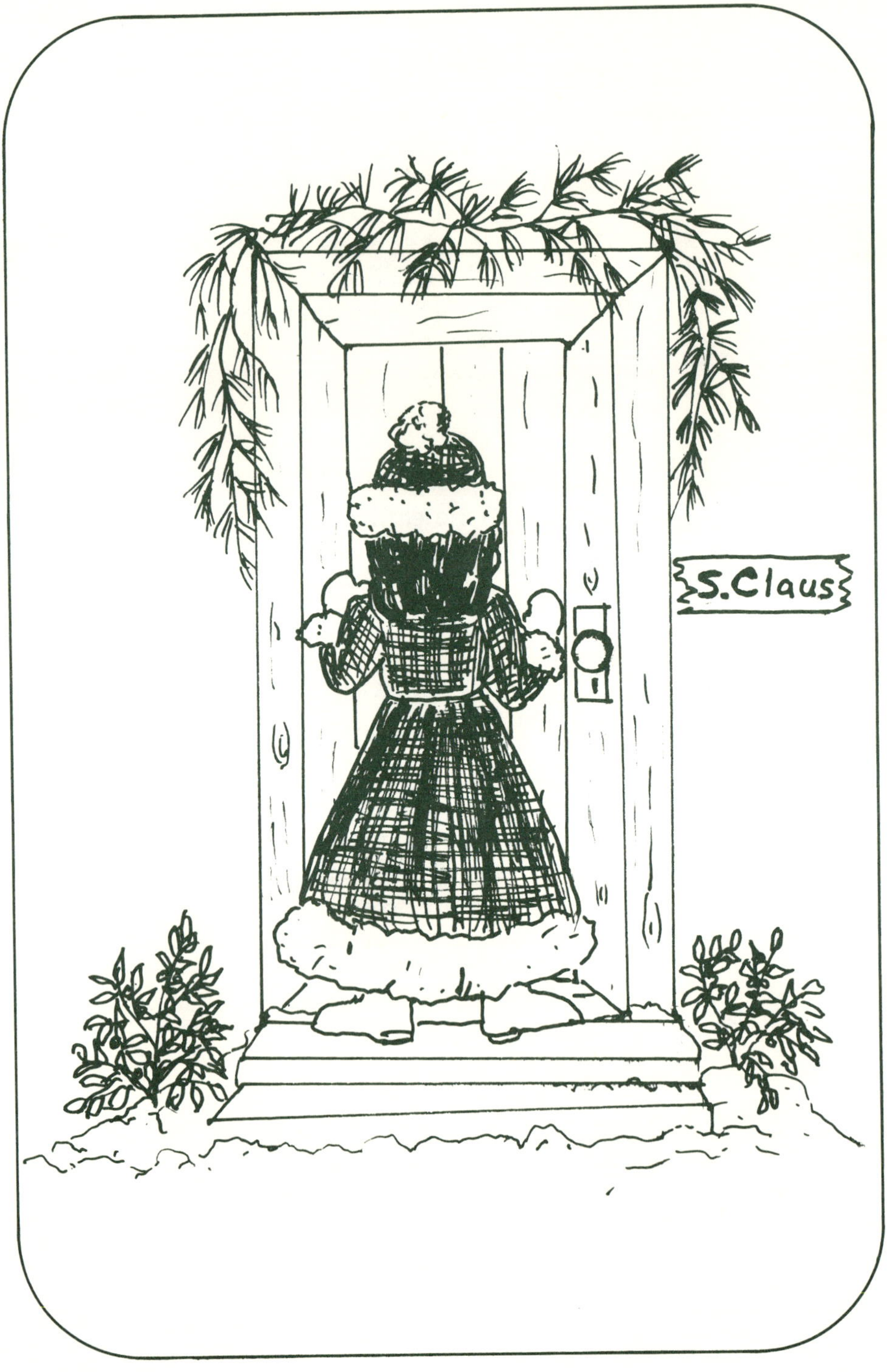
S.Claus

Santa opened all the gifts;
The big ones and the small,
Then Charity said, "Santa,
I've no gift to give at all."

"I've nothing left to give you
But all my love and this . . ."
Then Charity gave Santa
A great big hug and kiss.

Santa answered, "Charity,
I'm very proud of you.
I've heard of all the deeds you've done,
How giving you are, too."

"To have you in my house today
Is truly to be blessed,
For there's no greater gift than love.
The gift you gave is *best!*"

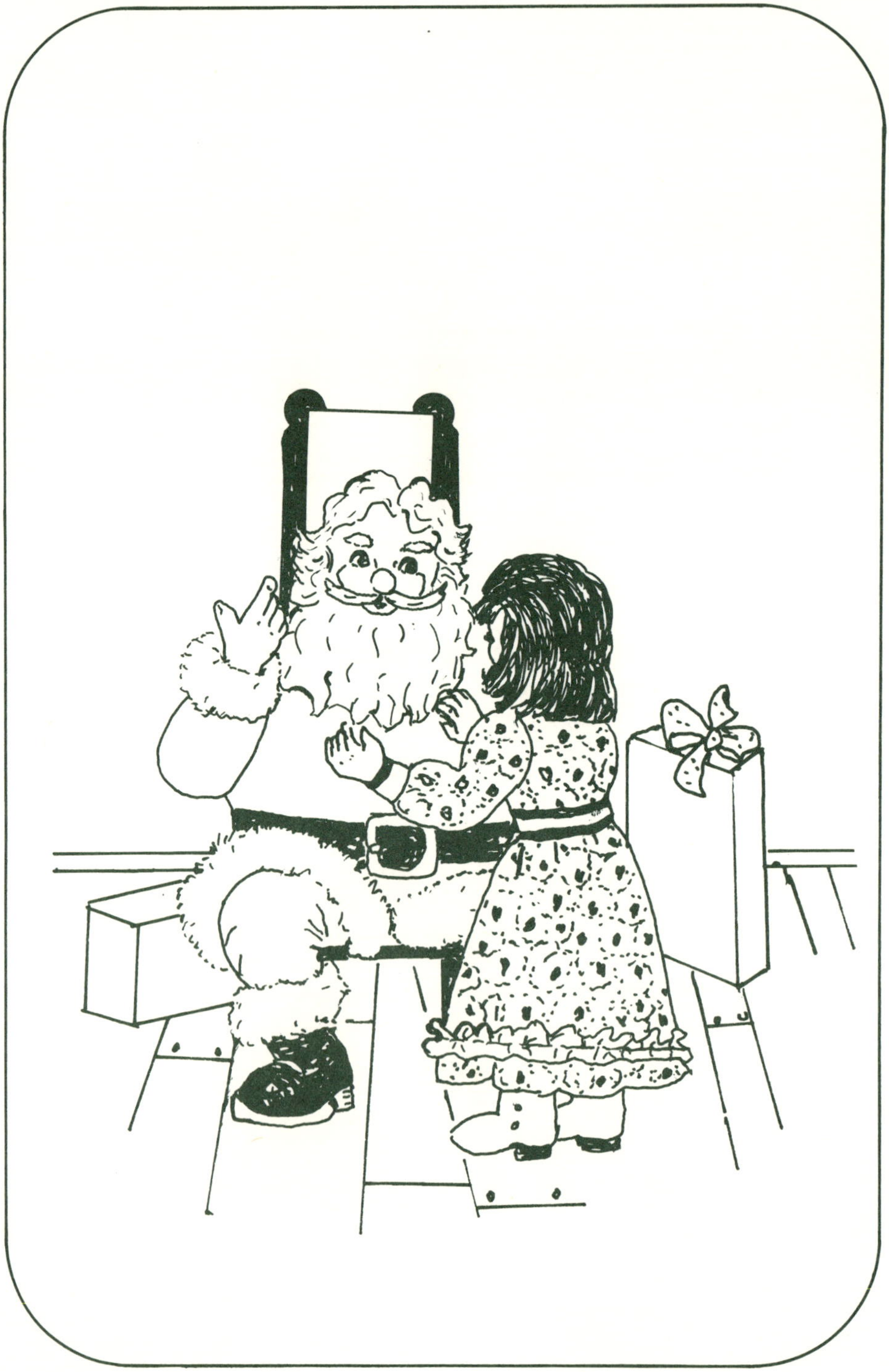

CHRISTMAS FAVORITES

From Little Town of Bethlehem

O holy Child of Bethlehem!
   Descend to us, we pray;
Cast out our sin, and enter in—
   Be born in us to-day.
            —Phillips Brooks

From Hark, the Glad Sound

Our glad Hosannas, Prince of Peace,
   Thy welcome shall proclaim,
And heaven's eternal arches ring
   With Thy belovèd name.
            —Philip Doddridge

From Christmas

O Father, May that holy star
   Grow every year more bright,
And send its glorious beams afar
   To fill the world with light.
        —William Cullen Bryant

From In the Bleak Midwinter

What can I give Him,
   Poor as I am?
If I were a shepherd
I would bring a lamb;
If I were a Wise Man
   I would do my part;
Yet what can I give Him—
   Give my heart.
        —Christina G. Rossetti

From Shepherds, Rejoice

Lord! and shall angels have their songs,
   And men no tunes to raise?
O may we lose these useless tongues
   When they forget to praise!

Glory to God that reigns above,
   That pitied us, forlorn!
We join to sing our Maker's love—
   For there's a savior born!
        —Isaac Watts

From Christmas

Here comes old Father Christmas,
 With sound of fife and drums;
With mistletoe about his brow,
 So merrily he comes!
—Rose Terry Cooke

From At the Sign of the Jolly Jack

Be ye merry and make good cheer,
For Christmas comes but once a year;
Scrape the fiddle and beat the drum,
And bury the night ere morning come.
—Geoffrey Smith

From Holly Song (from *As You Like It*)

Heigh-ho! sing, heigh-ho! unto the green holly:
Most friendship is feigning, most loving mere folly:
 Then, heigh-ho, the holly!
  This life is most jolly.
—William Shakespeare

Yes, Virginia, There Is a Santa Claus!

This answer to, "Is There a Santa Claus?" first appeared in the *New York Sun,* September 21, 1897. It was written by newspaperman Francis Pharcellus Church.

Dear Editor:
I am 8 years old.
Some of my little friends say there is no Santa Claus.
Papa says "If you see it in *The Sun* it's so."
Please tell me the truth, is there a Santa Claus?
Virginia O'Hanlon
115 West 95th Street

Virginia, your little friends are wrong. They have been affected by the skepticism of a skeptical age. They do not believe except they see. They think that nothing can be which is not comprehensible by their little minds. All minds, Virginia, whether they be men's or children's are little. In this great universe of ours man is a mere insect, an ant, in his intellect, as compared with the boundless world about him, as measured by the intelligence capable of grasping the whole of truth and knowledge.

Yes, Virginia, there is a Santa Claus. He exists as certainly as love and generosity and devotion exist, and you know that they abound and give to your life its highest beauty and joy. Alas! how dreary would be the world if there were no Santa Claus! It would be as dreary as if there were no Virginias. There would be no childlike faith then, no poetry, no romance to make tolerable this existence. We should have no enjoyment, except in sense and sight. The eternal light with which childhood fills the world would be extinguished.

Not believe in Santa Claus! You might as well not believe in fairies! You might get your papa to hire men to watch in all the chimneys on Christmas eve to catch Santa Claus, but even if they did not see Santa Claus coming down, what would that prove? Nobody sees Santa Claus, but that is no sign that there is no Santa Claus. The most real things in the world are those that neither children nor men can see. Did you ever see fairies dancing on the lawn? Of course not, but that's no proof that they are not there. Nobody can conceive or imagine all the wonders there are unseen and unseeable in the world.

You tear apart a baby's rattle and see what makes the noise

inside, but there is a veil covering the unseen world which not the strongest man, not even the united strength of all the strongest men that ever lived, could tear apart. Only faith, fancy, poetry, love, romance, can push aside that curtain and view and picture the supernal beauty and glory beyond. Is it all real? Ah, Virginia, in all this world there is nothing else real and abiding.

No Santa Claus! Thank God he lives, and he lives forever. A thousand years from now, Virginia, nay, ten times ten thousand years from now, he will continue to make glad the heart of childhood.

A Visit from St. Nicholas

'Twas the night before Christmas, when all through the house
Not a creature was stirring, not even a mouse;
The stockings were hung by the chimney with care,
In hopes that St. Nicholas soon would be there;
The children were nestled all snug in their beds,
While visions of sugar-plums danced in their heads;
And mamma in her kerchief, and I in my cap,
Had just settled our brains for a long winter's nap—
When out on the lawn there arose such a clatter,
I sprang from my bed to see what was the matter.
Away to the window I flew like a flash,
Tore open the shutters and threw up the sash.
The moon on the breast of the new-fallen snow
Gave a lustre of midday to objects below;
When what to my wondering eyes should appear,
But a miniature sleigh and eight tiny reindeer,
With a little old driver, so lively and quick
I knew in a moment it must be St. Nick!
More rapid than eagles his coursers they came,
And he whistled and shouted, and called them by name:
"Now, Dasher! now, Dancer! now, Prancer and Vixen!
On, Comet! on, Cupid! on, Donder and Blitzen!
To the top of the porch, to the top of the wall!
Now dash away, dash away, dash away all!"
As dry leaves that before the wild hurricane fly,
When they meet with an obstacle, mount to the sky,
So up to the house-top the coursers they flew,
With the sleigh full of toys—and St. Nicholas, too.
And then in a twinkling I heard on the roof
The prancing and pawing of each little hoof.
As I drew my head, and was turning around,
Down the chimney St. Nicholas came with a bound.
He was dressed all in fur from his head to his foot,
And his clothes were all tarnished with ashes and soot;

A bundle of toys he had flung on his back,
And he looked like a peddler just opening his pack.
His eyes, how they twinkled! his dimples, how merry!
His cheeks were like roses, his nose like a cherry;
His droll little mouth was drawn up like a bow,
And the beard on his chin was as white as the snow.
The stump of a pipe he held tight in his teeth,
And the smoke it encircled his head like a wreath.
He had a broad face and a little round belly
That shook, when he laughed, like a bowl full of jelly.
He was chubby and plump—a right jolly old elf;
And I laughed, when I saw him, in spite of myself.
A wink of his eye and a twist of his head
Soon gave me to know I had nothing to dread.
He spoke not a word, but went straight to his work,
And filled all the stockings; then turned with a jerk,
And laying his finger aside of his nose,
And giving a nod, up the chimney he rose.
He sprang in his sleigh, to his team gave a whistle,
And away they all flew like the down of a thistle;
But I heard him exclaim, ere he drove out of sight:
"Happy Christmas to all, and to all a good-night!"

—Clement C. Moore

The Mahogany Tree

Christmas is here;
Winds whistle shrill,
Icy and chill,
Little care we:
Little we fear
Weather without,
Sheltered about
The mahogany tree.

Once on the boughs,
Birds of rare plume
Sang, in its bloom;
Night birds are we:
Here we carouse,
Singing like them,
Perched round the stem
Of the jolly old tree.

Here let us sport,
Boys, as we sit;
Laughter and wit
Flashing so free.
Life is but short—
When we are gone,
Let them sing on,
Round the old tree.

Evenings we knew,
Happy as this;
Faces we miss,
Pleasant to see,
Kind hearts and true,
Gentle and just,
Peace to your dust!
We sing round the tree.

Care, like a dun,
Lurks at the gate:
Let the dog wait:
Happy we'll be!
Drink, every one;
Pile up the coals,
Fill the red bowls,
Round the old tree!

Drain we the cup—
Friend, art afraid?
Spirits are laid
In the Red Sea.
Mantle it up;
Empty it yet;
Let us forget,
Round the old tree.

Sorrows, begone!
Life and its ills,
Duns and their bills,
Bid we to flee.
Come with the dawn,
Blue-devil sprite,
Leave us to-night,
Round the old tree.

—W. M. Thackeray

Peace on Earth

I heard the bells on Christmas Day
Their old, familiar carols play,
   And wild and sweet
   The words repeat,
Of peace on earth, good-will to men!

And thought how, as the day had come,
The belfries of all Christendom
   Had rolled along
   The unbroken song
Of peace on earth, good-will to men!

Till, ringing, singing on its way,
The world revolved from night to day,
   A voice, a chime,
   A chant sublime
Of peace on earth, good-will to men!

Then from each black, accursed mouth
The cannon thundered in the South,
   And with the sound
   The carols drowned
Of peace on earth, good-will to men!

It was as if an earthquake rent
The hearthstones of a continent,
   And made forlorn
   The households born
Of peace on earth, good-will to men!

And in despair I bowed my head;
"There is no peace on earth," I said;
  "For hate is strong,
  And mocks the song
Of peace on earth, good-will to men!"

Then pealed the bells more loud and deep:
"God is not dead, nor doth He sleep!
  The Wrong shall fail,
  The Right prevail,
With peace on earth, good-will to men!"

—Henry W. Longfellow

A Lullaby for Christmas

Sleep, baby, sleep! The mother sings:
Heaven's angels kneel and fold their wings.
   Sleep, baby, sleep!

Sleep, baby, sleep! The father cries:
Stars lean and worship from the skies.
   Sleep, baby, sleep!

With swathes of scented hay Thy bed
By Mary's hand at eve was spread.
   Sleep, baby, sleep!

At midnight came the shepherds, they
Whom angels wakened by the way.
   Sleep, baby, sleep!

And three kings from the East afar,
Ere dawn, came, guided by Thy star.
   Sleep, baby, sleep!

They brought Thee gifts of gold and gems,
Pure Orient pearls, rich diadems.
   Sleep, baby, sleep!

But Thou, who liest slumbering there,
Art King of kings, earth, stars, and air.
   Sleep, baby, sleep!

Sleep, baby, sleep! The shepherds sing:
Through earth, through heaven, hosannas ring.
   Sleep, baby, sleep!

—John Addington Symonds

Cradle Hymn

Away in a manger, no crib for a bed,
The little Lord Jesus laid down His sweet head.
The stars in the bright sky looked down where He lay—
The little Lord Jesus asleep on the hay.

The cattle are lowing, the Baby awakes,
But little Lord Jesus no crying He makes,
I love thee, Lord Jesus! Look down from the sky.
And stay by my cradle till morning is nigh.

—Martin Luther

Hark! the Herald Angels

Hark! the herald angels sing,
"Glory to the new-born King!
Peace on earth and mercy mild,
God and sinners reconciled!"
Christ, by highest heaven adored,
Christ, the everlasting Lord,
Late in time behold Him come,
Offspring of a Virgin's womb.
   Hark! the herald angels sing,
   Glory to the new-born King!

Veiled in flesh the Godhead see;
Hail the incarnate Deity!
Pleased as man with men to appear,
Jesus our Immanuel here.
Hail the heaven-born Prince of Peace!
Hail the Son of Righteousness!
Light and life to all He brings,
Risen with healing in His wings.
   Hark! the herald angels sing,
   Glory to the new-born King!

Mild He lays His glory by,
Born that man no more may die;
Born to raise the sons of earth,
Born to give them second birth.
Come, Desire of nations, come,
Fix in us Thy humble home;
Rise, the woman's conquering Seed,
Bruise in us the serpent's head.
   Hark! the herald angels sing,
   Glory to the new-born King!

Adam's likeness now efface,
Stamp Thine image in its place;
Second Adam from above,
Reinstate us in Thy love.
Hark! the herald angels sing,
"Glory to the new-born King!
Peace on earth, and mercy mild,
God and sinners reconciled!"
  Hark! the herald angels sing,
  Glory to the new-born King!

—Charles Wesley

The Shepherds Had an Angel

The Shepherds had an Angel,
  The Wise Men had a star,
But what have I, a little child,
  To guide me home from far,
Where glad stars sing together,
  And singing Angels are?

Lord Jesus is my Guardian,
  So I can nothing lack:
The lambs lie in His bosom
  Along life's dangerous track:
The wilful lambs that go astray
  He bleeding fetches back.

Lord Jesus is my guiding star,
  My beacon light in heaven:
He leads me step by step along
  The path of life uneven:
He, true light, leads me to that land
  Whose day shall be as seven.

Those Shepherds through the lonely night
  Sat watching by their sheep,
Until they saw the heavenly host,
  Who neither tire nor sleep,
All singing "Glory, glory,"
  In festival they keep.

Christ watches me, His little lamb;
  Cares for me day and night,
That I may be His own in heaven:
  So angels, clad in white,
Shall sing their "Glory, glory"
  For my sake in the height.

The Wise Men left their country
   To journey morn by morn,
With gold and frankincense and myrrh,
   Because the Lord was born:
God sent a star to guide them
   And sent a dream to warn.

My life is like their journey,
   Their star is like God's book;
I must be like those good Wise Men
   With heavenward heart and look:
But shall I give no gifts to God?
   What precious gifts they took!

Lord, I will give my love to Thee,
   Than gold much costlier,
Sweeter to Thee than frankincense,
   More prized than choicest myrrh;
Lord, make me dearer day by day,
   Day by day holier;

Nearer and dearer day by day,
   Till I my voice unite,
And sing my "Glory, glory"
   With angels clad in white;
All "Glory, glory" given to Thee
   Through all the heavenly height.

            —Christina G. Rossetti

PART 2
Love from the Kitchen

The kitchen's been busy.
It smells quite delicious.
The whole gang is coming
To savor new dishes;
And they each get a tin
Of cookies and sweets,
For everyone treasures
Those holiday treats!

APPETIZERS AND SOUPS

Cheese Trees

½ cup soft butter or margarine
⅓ cup grated sharp Cheddar cheese (or any other grated hard cheese you desire)
⅔ cup flour

½ teaspoon baking powder
1 egg
1 teaspoon poppy seeds
½ teaspoon seasoning salt

Preheat oven to 350°. Add cheese to soft butter or margarine. Blend in flour, baking powder, egg, poppy seeds, and seasoning salt. Mix well. Using a cookie press with a tree design, form into trees on an ungreased cookie sheet. Bake 8 to 10 minutes. Be careful not to over-brown. Remove from pan. Cool. Makes about 30 trees.

Onion Soup au Gratin

2 tablespoons chicken bouillon
2 tablespoons beef bouillon
2 quarts water
1½ pounds onion
4 tablespoons butter

¼ teaspoon pepper
1 bay leaf
8 slices mozzarella cheese
8 slices French bread
salt to taste

Peel and slice onions in ¼-inch slices. Sauté in butter until they begin to brown. Add pepper, bouillons, and bay leaf. Stir to blend. Add to boiling water. Simmer for 30 minutes and remove bay leaf. Pour soup into individual serving sized oven-proof soup crocks. Top each with a slice of dry-toasted French bread. Top with cheese. Place under broiler until cheese melts and begins to brown. Makes 8 servings.

Vegy-Cheese Soup

3 cups water
4 teaspoons instant chicken bouillon
1 large potato
2 large onions, chopped
½ cup chopped carrots
½ cup chopped celery
2 cups shredded Cheddar or American cheese
1 teaspoon salt
¼ teaspoon white pepper
1 cup half-and-half

In a 3-quart saucepan boil instant chicken bouillon in water. Chop all vegetables very fine. Add to broth mixture, cover, and simmer until vegetables are tender, about 15 minutes. Stir in remaining ingredients. Heat till cheese melts (do not boil). Makes 6 to 8 servings.

Lentil Soup

12 cups beef stock
8 ounces dried lentils
1 small potato, diced
4 celery stalks, diced
2 large carrots, diced
1 large onion, diced
½ pound weiners, sliced
salt and pepper

Bring stock to boil in large saucepan. Add lentils and other vegetables and boil until tender, 2 hours. Reduce heat and add sliced weiners. Cook 30 minutes, stirring frequently. Salt and pepper to taste. Makes 6 to 8 servings.

Clam Chowder

1 medium onion, chopped
2 small potatoes, peeled
   and chopped
1 small carrot, peeled
   and chopped
2 stalks of celery, chopped

2 tablespoons butter
3 cups chicken broth
2 7-ounce cans minced clams
1 16-ounce can of tomatoes,
   drained and chopped
salt and pepper to taste

Sauté onion, potatoes, carrot, and celery in butter. Pour chicken broth in 2-quart pan, add sautéed vegetables and all other ingredients. Bring to boil. Cover and simmer for 20 minutes. Season with salt and pepper. Serve hot. Makes 4 servings.

Chicken Liver Pâté

1 pound chicken livers
¼ cup vegetable oil

1 pouch onion soup mix
2 hard-boiled eggs

Sauté chicken livers in small amount of vegetable oil. Put sautéed livers, soup mix, hard-boiled eggs, and vegetable oil in blender or food processor. Blend until smooth. Chill, shape, and garnish. Serves 8 to 12.

Spinach-Onion Dip

1 pouch onion soup mix
1 cup sour cream
1 cup plain yogurt
1 10-ounce package frozen chopped spinach, defrosted and well drained

In a medium bowl blend all ingredients. Cover and chill at least 2 hours. Serve as a dip for chips or cut-up raw vegetables, or use as a sauce over plain cooked vegetables. Makes 2 cups.

Curry Dip

2 cups sour cream
1 pouch onion soup mix
½ teaspoon curry powder
¼ cup unsalted dry-roasted peanuts, finely chopped

Blend all ingredients in medium bowl. Cover and chill 2 hours. Serve with crisp vegetables, corn chips, or potato chips. Makes 2 cups.

Cucumber and Dill Dip

1 medium cucumber
⅛ teaspoon dillweed
1 teaspoon lemon juice
⅛ teaspoon salt
dash of pepper
2 cups sour cream

Peel and grate cucumber, coarse. Combine with all other ingredients. Chill and serve with vegetables in season.

Stuffed Cherry Tomatoes

½ cup finely chopped ham or turkey
2 teaspoons mayonnaise
1 teaspoon pickle relish
2 dozen cherry tomatoes

Mix ham or turkey with mayonnaise and relish. Set aside. Cut tops off cherry tomatoes. Remove pulp. Drain shells upside down on paper towels. Stuff tomatoes with ham or turkey mixture. Chill. Makes 24 appetizers.

ENTRÉES

Baked Ham with Dijon Sauce

6 to 7 pounds cooked ham
2 tablespoons Dijon mustard
½ cup orange juice
⅓ cup brown sugar

Preheat oven to 325°. Cut off and discard skin from ham. Lay ham, fat side up, in shallow pan. Roast uncovered for 1 hour. Remove from oven. Score fat with diagonal cuts, making diamond shapes. In a small bowl blend mustard, juice, and sugar. Brush half the sauce over ham. Continue roasting uncovered for 45 minutes or until glaze is brown and baste often with remaining sauce. Serves about 10.

Scalloped Ham and Potatoes

3 cups diced cooked ham
4 cups thinly sliced peeled potatoes
1 cup chopped onion
1 10¾-ounce can condensed mushroom soup
½ teaspoon salt
⅛ teaspoon pepper
¼ cup grated cheese

Preheat oven to 375°. Grease 3-quart casserole. Arrange ham and potatoes in alternate layers. Mix all other ingredients and pour sauce over ham and potatoes. Cover and bake for 45 minutes. Remove cover and bake for 30 more minutes. Serves 8.

Turkey Roast Supreme

1 frozen turkey roast, 4 to 4½ pounds
1 cup chicken broth
3 tablespoons butter or margarine
¼ teaspoon seasoned salt
2 tablespoons flour or 1 tablespoon cornstarch
¼ cup water
½ cup apple jelly
¼ cup raisins
1 jar apple rings

Preheat oven to 350°. Place thawed turkey roast, skin side up, in roasting pan. In a small saucepan, heat chicken broth and stir in butter or margarine and seasoned salt. Pour over turkey roast and cover. Roast 1½ hours, basting frequently. Remove cover and continue roasting for 1 hour or until roast is lightly browned. Remove roast from pan. Pour liquid from pan into measuring cup and add water to make 1 cup. Return liquid to pan and bring to a boil. In a cup, add water slowly to flour to make a smooth paste, stir into boiling water liquid in pan. Cook until liquid begins to thicken; add apple jelly and raisins. Continue cooking until gravy thickens. Place roast on heated serving platter garnished with apple rings. Serve gravy separately.

Turkey Tetrazzini

1 10¾-ounce can condensed cream of mushroom soup
½ cup milk
2 cups cooked turkey cut into small cubes
6 ounces broad noodles, cooked and drained
¼ cup grated Parmesan cheese

Preheat oven to 350°. Grease a 2-quart baking dish. Mix soup and milk. Add remaining ingredients except cheese. Mix gently. Pour into prepared baking dish and sprinkle with cheese. Bake 25 to 30 minutes. Makes 4 servings.

Curried Turkey Salad

½ cup chopped green onion
1 teaspoon curry powder
½ teaspoon salt
¼ teaspoon pepper
¾ cup mayonnaise or
　salad dressing
1 10-ounce package frozen peas,
　cooked and cooled
4 cups diced turkey
lettuce leaves
cherry tomatoes

Mix onions, curry powder, salt, pepper, and mayonnaise. Add peas and turkey; mix well. Refrigerate covered for 2 hours or longer. To serve, mound salad over lettuce leaves and top with a cherry tomato. Serves 8 to 10.

Turkey Meatballs with Sweet and Sour Sauce

Meatballs:
1½ pounds ground turkey
1 egg, beaten
½ cup breadcrumbs
½ teaspoon onion salt
½ teaspoon salt
¼ cup oil

Combine all ingredients except oil. Shape into 1-inch meatballs. In a 12-inch skillet, heat oil over medium heat; add meatballs and brown on all sides. Remove meatballs and serve with toothpicks around sauce.

Sauce:
1 16-ounce can jellied
　cranberry sauce
2 tablespoons honey
1 tablespoon lemon juice
1 tablespoon Worcestershire
　sauce

In a medium saucepan combine all ingredients, bring to a boil, cover and simmer for 5 minutes. Makes about 1½ cups.

Shepherd's Pie

1 pound ground pork or beef
¼ cup chopped onion
4 slices bacon cut into small pieces
1 teaspoon salt
1 cup tomato juice

2 tablespoons flour or 1 tablespoon cornstarch
¼ cup water
1 egg
2 cups seasoned mashed potatoes

Preheat oven to 350°. Grease 2-quart casserole. Brown meat, onion, and bacon in skillet. Add salt and tomato juice. Simmer for 15 minutes. Add flour to water, stirring to make a smooth paste; add to meat. Add egg to mashed potatoes, mix well, and press potatoes in casserole as a crust. Cover potatoes with meat mixture. Bake uncovered for 30 minutes. Serves 4 to 6.

Deep Dish Lamb Stew

2 pounds boneless lamb, cubed
2 tablespoons salad oil
1 cup chopped onion
2 cups chicken broth
½ teaspoon salt

⅛ teaspoon pepper
1 cup sliced celery
1 cup cut carrots
1 10-ounce package frozen peas
2 tablespoons mashed potatoes
1 package refrigerator biscuits

Brown lamb in oil, add onion and sauté till onion is clear. Add chicken broth, salt, and pepper and simmer for 30 minutes. Add celery, carrots, and peas, simmer for 30 minutes or until meat and carrots are tender. In a small cup make a paste from the lamb stew gravy and mashed potatoes. Mix paste into stew and continue cooking till gravy thickens. Turn stew into a 2-quart casserole, cover with biscuits and bake at 400° until biscuits are browned. Serves 6 to 8.

Italian Swiss Steak

2 pounds round steak, cut into 6 or 8 servings
1 medium-sized zucchini
1 cup sliced carrots
1 envelope dry onion soup mix
½ teaspoon Italian spice mix
1 15-ounce can tomato sauce

In a large skillet or Dutch oven, arrange meat; surround with vegetables. Mix onion soup, spices, and tomato sauce; pour over meat and vegetables. Cover and roast in 325° oven for 3 to 3½ hours or until meat is tender and sauce is thick. Serves 6 to 8.

Stroganoff Meatballs

1 pound ground beef
1 egg, beaten
1 teaspoon seasoning salt
⅓ cup milk
½ cup uncooked oatmeal
3 tablespoons vegetable oil
1 6-ounce can mushrooms
1 8-ounce package noodles
2 cups sour cream

Combine meat, egg, seasoning salt, milk, and oatmeal. Mix thoroughly. Shape into 24 meatballs. Brown in vegetable oil. Drain off oil and add canned mushrooms with their liquid. Cover and simmer for 20 minutes. While meatballs are cooking, prepare noodles according to directions. Add sour cream to meatballs and mushrooms, heat thoroughly. Arrange hot drained noodles on serving dish. Pour stroganoff mixture over top and serve. Makes about 6 servings.

Frosted Meat Loaf

1½ pounds ground beef
1 small onion, chopped
½ cup bread crumbs
1 teaspoon salt
1 tablespoon Worcestershire sauce
½ cup milk
1 egg, beaten
4 cups whipped potatoes
4 stuffed green olives, sliced

Preheat oven to 350°. Combine all ingredients except whipped potatoes and olives. Pack meat loaf into loaf pan. Bake for 1 hour. Remove from oven and let stand for a few minutes, then remove

LOVE FROM THE KITCHEN ~ 77

meat loaf from pan and place on a cookie sheet. Spread whipped potatoes over top and sides of meat loaf, garnish with olive slices. Broil 5 minutes about 3 inches from source of heat. Transfer to a serving platter. Makes 6 to 8 servings.

Ham and Cheese Quiche

1 cup chopped ham
1 cup shredded Swiss cheese
1 9-inch pie shell, lightly baked
4 eggs
1 cup milk
½ teaspoon salt

Preheat oven to 375°. Sprinkle ham and cheese into pie shell. Beat together eggs, milk, and salt. Pour over ham and cheese. Bake 35 to 40 minutes. Knife inserted near center should come out clean. Let stand a few minutes before cutting. Makes 6 servings.

Hearty Meatballs and Cabbage

1 medium cabbage, about 1½ pounds
1 cup sliced carrots
2 pounds lean ground beef
¼ cup quick cooking rice, uncooked
2 eggs, beaten
½ teaspoon seasoned salt
1 16-ounce can or package sauerkraut
½ teaspoon salt
1 cup catsup
2 15-ounce cans tomato sauce

Preheat oven to 350°. Coarsely shred cabbage. Put cabbage and carrots in bottom of large casserole, or Dutch oven. Mix ground beef, rice, eggs and seasoned salt. Shape meat into 16 meatballs; put on top of cabbage. Mix sauerkraut, salt, catsup, and tomato sauce. Pour sauce over other ingredients. Cover and bake for 3 hours, or until sauce thickens. Makes 8 to 12 servings.

Barbecued Pot Roast

4 pounds boneless beef roast
¼ cup tomato juice
¾ cup barbecue sauce
1 cup chopped green peppers
1 cup chopped onion
salt to taste

Place beef roast in roasting pan. Mix together the rest of the ingredients and pour over roast. Cover and roast at 350° for 3½ to 4 hours, basting frequently. Turn off oven and remove cover so sauce will brown on meat. Slice and serve with sauce. Serves 8 to 10.

Zesty Chicken Breasts

⅓ cup mayonnaise
1 teaspoon seasoned salt
⅛ teaspoon pepper
4 skinned chicken breast fillets
⅔ cup cornflake crumbs

Preheat oven to 375°. Grease shallow baking pan. Blend mayonnaise with seasoned salt and pepper. Brush both sides of chicken breasts with mixture. Coat with cornflake crumbs. Place in baking pan and bake for 25 to 30 minutes. Serves 4.

Ginger Chicken Salad

3 cups cooked chicken, cubed
½ cup chopped celery
1 cup unpeeled tart apples, cubed
½ cup chopped walnuts
¾ cup mayonnaise or salad dressing
½ teaspoon ground ginger
1 teaspoon lemon juice
½ teaspoon salt

Combine chicken, celery, apples, and walnuts in a large bowl. Blend mayonnaise or salad dressing, ginger, lemon juice, and salt in a small bowl. Spoon over other ingredients. Mix well and chill. Serves 6 to 8.

LOVE FROM THE KITCHEN

SALADS AND SIDE DISHES

Vegetables au Gratin

¼ cup grated American cheese
1 10¾-ounce can condensed cream of mushroom soup
2 cups crisp-tender cooked cauliflower
2 cups crisp-tender cooked broccoli
½ cup coarse cracker crumbs
2 tablespoons butter or margarine

Preheat oven to 350°. Grease 1-quart casserole. Blend grated cheese into soup. Combine vegetables and put mixture into casserole. Sprinkle with crumbs and dot with butter. Bake 20 minutes. Serves 8.

Glazed Carrots

6 medium-sized carrots, pared and sliced lengthwise
¼ cup light brown sugar
¼ cup butter

Cook carrots until barely tender, about 10 minutes. Drain. Add brown sugar and butter to saucepan. Continue cooking until a glaze is formed. Serves 4.

Cheese Potato Balls

2 cups cold mashed potatoes
1 egg, beaten
⅓ cup grated cheese
½ cup crushed cornflakes
2 tablespoons butter

Preheat oven to 425°. Grease baking sheet. Mix potatoes, egg, and cheese. Shape into 4 balls. Roll each ball in crushed cornflakes. Dot each ball with butter and place on baking sheet. Bake 20 minutes. Serves 4.

Walnut Candied Sweet Potatoes

½ cup brown sugar
¼ cup water
2 tablespoons butter
¼ teaspoon salt
8 to 10 cooked sweet potatoes
½ cup walnuts

Combine sugar, water, butter, and salt. Pour over potatoes in saucepan. Cook for 20 minutes. Add nuts and serve. Serves 8 to 10.

Scalloped Spinach and Pimiento

2 10-ounce packages frozen chopped spinach, cooked and drained
¾ cup milk
3 beaten eggs
¾ cup shredded American cheese
1 tablespoon chopped pimiento
½ teaspoon onion salt
⅛ teaspoon white pepper
1 cup cracker crumbs
1 tablespoon melted margarine or butter

Preheat oven to 350°. Grease an 8 x 8 x 2-inch pan. Mix cooked spinach with milk, eggs, ½ cup shredded cheese, pimiento, onion salt, and pepper. Put into pan. Bake for 25 minutes. Combine crumbs, ¼ cup cheese, and margarine and sprinkle on spinach. Bake 10 to 15 minutes longer. Let stand 5 minutes before serving. Makes 6 servings.

Grandma's Red Cabbage

1 medium head of red
  cabbage, shredded
2 medium apples, peeled
  and chopped
½ cup vinegar

½ cup water
½ cup brown sugar
1 teaspoon salt
dash of pepper
1 tablespoon salad oil

Mix all ingredients together. Simmer in a covered pot for 1 hour. Makes 6 to 8 servings.

Wax Beans and Bacon

4 slices bacon, cut in pieces
½ cup coarsely chopped onion
4 cups canned or cooked wax beans (or green beans)
½ teaspoon salt
¼ teaspoon pepper

Fry bacon until crisp. Remove from fat and crumble. Cook onion in bacon fat until slightly browned. Add beans, salt, and pepper. Stir until heated. Add crumbled bacon and serve. Makes 6 servings.

Red and Green Coleslaw

1 cup sour cream
1 tablespoon salad dressing or mayonnaise
1 teaspoon celery seed
½ teaspoon salt
¼ teaspoon pepper
2 tablespoons vinegar
2 tablespoons sugar
5 cups finely shredded red and green cabbage
1 cup peeled and shredded carrots

To make the slaw dressing, mix together all ingredients except the cabbage and carrots. Pour dressing over the cabbage and carrots. Mix well. Serves 6 to 8.

Tomato Aspic

1 package (4-serving size) lemon flavored gelatin, regular or sugar-free
1 cup boiling water
1 8-ounce can tomato sauce
1 teaspoon Worcestershire sauce
⅛ teaspoon red pepper sauce
1 cup green vegetables (celery, peas, broccoli florets)

Mix gelatin and boiling water until gelatin is dissolved. Add tomato sauce and seasonings. Pour into a 4-cup mold. Chill until slightly thickened. Add vegetables and chill until firm. To serve, loosen edge of mold with knife. Lift mold quickly in and out of pot or bowl containing hot tap water. Put serving plate on top of mold and flip; remove mold carefully. Makes 6 to 8 servings.

Marinated Snow Peas and Carrots

1 20-ounce package frozen carrot slices
1 8-ounce package frozen snow peas
¼ cup lemon juice
2 tablespoons vegetable oil
½ teaspoon salt
⅛ teaspoon pepper
½ teaspoon dried dillweed
1 tablespoon chopped red onion

Cook carrots and snow peas to a crisp-tender stage. Mix all other ingredients in a medium-sized bowl. Stir in vegetables. Cover and refrigerate at least 6 hours or up to two days. Stir occasionally. Makes 6 to 8 servings.

Creamy Hot Potato Salad

1 10¾-ounce can condensed cream of celery soup
1 teaspoon white vinegar
⅛ teaspoon pepper

¼ teaspoon salt
¼ cup chopped red onion
¼ cup chopped green pepper
3 tablespoons sweet-pickle relish
4 slices bacon, cooked and crumbled
2 pounds unpeeled small red potatoes, cooked and quartered

Heat soup. Mix with all ingredients except bacon and potatoes. Add hot potatoes; mix until coated. Garnish with crumbled bacon. Serve warm. Makes 4 servings.

Frozen Cranberry-Orange Salad

1 4-serving size orange flavored gelatin, regular or sugar-free
1 cup boiling water
1 11-ounce can mandarin orange sections
½ cup chopped nuts
1 14-ounce jar cranberry-orange sauce
lettuce leaves
mayonnaise or whipped cream (optional)

Dissolve gelatin in boiling water. Drain but reserve syrup of mandarin oranges. Add water to syrup for ¾-cup cold liquid. Add to gelatin. Add nuts, cranberry-orange sauce, and oranges. Pour into 8x8-inch pan. Freeze for 3 hours or until firm. Put into refrigerator for 30 minutes before serving. Slice and serve on lettuce. May be garnished with mayonnaise or whipped cream topping. May also be used as a light dessert. Serves 4 to 6.

Spinach and Lettuce Salad

1 large bunch of spinach
1 medium head of lettuce
¼ cup sugar
1½ tablespoons chopped onion
1 cup oil
⅓ cup vinegar
1 teaspoon salt
1 teaspoon dry mustard
1½ cups large-curd cottage cheese
½ cup crumbled bacon

Wash and break apart spinach and lettuce. Mix together all other ingredients. Just before serving add the dressing to the greens. Makes 8 servings.

Five Bean Salad

    1 small onion
    1 small red bell pepper
    1 small green bell pepper
    1 16-ounce can red kidney beans, drained
    1 16-ounce can green lima beans, drained
    1 16-ounce can sliced green beans, drained
    1 16-ounce can wax white beans, drained
    1 16-ounce can chick peas, drained
    ¾ cup sugar
    1 teaspoon salt
    ½ teaspoon pepper
    ⅔ cup vinegar
    ⅓ cup corn oil

Dice onion and red and green peppers. Mix together with the five kinds of beans. Mix sugar, salt, pepper, vinegar, and oil together in saucepan. Bring sauce to a boil, and while hot, pour over beans. Cover, and when cool, refrigerate at least 6 hours, or up to two days. Stir occasionally. Makes 12 to 16 servings.

Christmas Antipasto

    1 pint cherry tomatoes, cut in halves
    1 package frozen Brussels sprouts, cooked and cooled
    ½ cup black olives, pitted
    ½ cup Italian salad dressing
    ½ cup sliced pepperoni
    ½ cup cubed cheese of your choice
    1 cup salad greens

Toss all ingredients but salad greens. Refrigerate. Just before serving add greens and toss. Serves 6 to 8.

Holiday Waldorf Salad

½ cup salad dressing or mayonnaise
½ cup prepared whipped cream topping
2 cups diced unpeeled apples
1 11-ounce can mandarin orange segments, drained
¼ cup raisins
¼ cup coarsely chopped nuts
lettuce leaves
Maraschino cherries (optional)
more nuts (optional)

Carefully fold salad dressing into whipped cream. Fold in the rest of the ingredients. Mound salad in lettuce cups. If desired, garnish with Maraschino cherry and nuts. Serves 7 or 8.

Honey-Cream Fruit Bowl

3 medium bananas
1 cup pitted dark sweet
  cherries, drained
2 medium oranges
1 medium grapefruit

½ cup sour cream
1 tablespoon honey
1 tablespoon salad dressing
  or mayonnaise

Slice peeled bananas into large bowl; cover with cherries. Peel, section, and remove membranes from oranges and grapefruit. Mix all fruits and chill. Meanwhile combine sour cream, honey, and salad dressing. Before serving, mix dressing with fruit. Makes 7 or 8 servings.

Double Corn Fritters

1 cup yellow cornmeal
1 cup flour
2 eggs
¼ cup shortening
4 teaspoons baking powder
½ teaspoon salt
½ cup milk
1 7- or 8-ounce can whole kernel corn, drained

Blend together all ingredients but corn. When batter is thoroughly mixed, add corn. Heat oil to 375° in deep fryer. Drop tablespoonfuls into hot oil and fry for about 5 minutes or till brown on both sides. Drain. Serves 8 to 10.

Corn Pudding

¼ cup flour
1 cup milk
1 egg
2 cups frozen or canned corn, drained
1 teaspoon salt
⅛ teaspoon pepper
½ teaspoon seasoned salt

Preheat oven to 350°. Mix flour and milk, slowly forming a thin paste. Add egg, beat. Mix in the rest of the ingredients. Pour into ungreased 1½-quart dish or casserole. Place in pan of hot water. Bake 1 to 1¼ hours or until knife inserted near the center comes out clean. Serve hot. Makes 6 servings.

Apple-Raisin-Rice Pudding

2 cups cooked rice
½ cup raisins
1 cup peeled diced apples
3 eggs, well beaten
4 cups milk
1 teaspoon cinnamon
½ cup sugar
¼ teaspoon salt

Preheat oven to 350°. Grease a 2-quart baking dish. Mix together all ingredients. Pour into baking dish. Bake 45 to 60 minutes, until pudding is set and lightly browned. Makes 8 servings.

Apricot Noodle Pudding

8 ounces cream cheese, at room temperature
1 cup apricot nectar juice
1 cup milk
3 large eggs
½ teaspoon vanilla
dash salt
6 ounces broad noodles, freshly cooked and drained
½ cup golden raisins

Heat oven to 350°. Grease a 2-quart square or oblong pan. Put all ingredients except noodles and raisins into blender or food processor. Mix till smooth. Fold in noodles and raisins. Pour mixture into greased pan. Bake 45 minutes, or until pudding is set and top is a golden brown. Let stand 10 minutes before serving. Makes 10 servings.

Wheat and Raisin Stuffing

2 loaves whole wheat bread
½ cup raisins
1 egg
½ cup melted butter or margarine
½ cup diced celery
1 cup chopped walnuts
1 teaspoon sage
½ teaspoon cinnamon

Toast bread on slow oven till it crumbles. Crumble bread into a large mixing bowl. Add enough water to moisten well; add raisins and let set. Beat egg, mix with margarine and rest of ingredients. Pour over bread mixture, stir well. Fill turkey cavity or bake in well-greased casserole at 375° for 30 minutes. Will stuff a 12- to 15-pound turkey. This dish is a good accompaniment to the turkey roast, page 74.

BREADS

Cheese Party Rye

1 loaf party rye bread
butter or margarine
Parmesan or Cheddar cheese

Heat oven to 350°. Spread slices of party rye bread with soft butter or margarine, then sprinkle with grated Parmesan or Cheddar cheese. Bake 10 to 12 minutes or until toasted.

Cranberry Muffins

1 egg
½ cup milk
¼ cup salad oil
1½ cups flour
½ cup sugar

2 teaspoons baking powder
½ teaspoon salt
½ teaspoon vanilla
¾ cup cranberry halves

Preheat oven to 400°. Grease or line 12 muffin cups. Beat egg with milk and oil. Mix in remaining ingredients until flour is moistened. Batter will be lumpy. Fill muffin cups ⅔ full. Bake 20 to 25 minutes. Serve warm.

Oatmeal Rolls

1 package yeast
¼ cup warm water
1 teaspoon sugar
1 cup scalded milk
⅓ cup sugar

⅓ cup salted butter or margarine
1 egg, beaten
3½ cups flour
1 cup uncooked oatmeal

Soften yeast in warm water and teaspoonful of sugar. Add scalded milk to ⅓ cup sugar and butter or margarine. Cool mixture slightly, then stir in egg and half the flour. Mix well, then add rest of flour and oatmeal to mixture. Turn out on lightly floured board and knead until satiny. Place dough in bowl, cover, and let rise about 1 hour, or until double in size. Divide dough and shape by placing in muffin cups or make roll shapes on cookie sheet. Cover and let rise for 45 minutes. Bake at 375° for 15 to 18 minutes. Makes 4 dozen rolls.

Banana Bread

½ cup butter or margarine
1½ cups sugar
½ teaspoon cinnamon
1 teaspoon vanilla
1 egg
1 teaspoon lemon juice

¼ cup milk
1 teaspoon baking soda
1½ cups flour
1 cup ripe mashed bananas
   (about 2 bananas)

Preheat oven to 350°. Grease 8-inch square pan. Cream butter or margarine, sugar, cinnamon, and vanilla, then add egg. Add lemon juice to milk, then add baking soda. To creamed mixture, add flour and milk mixture alternately, beating after each addition until smooth. Add bananas and mix thoroughly. Bake for 30 to 35 minutes.

Onion Hot Bread

½ cup soft butter or margarine
1 envelope onion soup mix
1 loaf French bread

Preheat oven to 400°. Cream butter or margarine together with onion soup mix. Cut bread into 1-inch slices and spread with mixture. Reassemble loaf. Wrap it securely in a piece of heavy-duty aluminum foil. Heat 15 to 20 minutes.

Zucchini Fruit Bread

1 cup sugar
1½ cups flour
1 teaspoon baking powder
1 teaspoon baking soda
1 teaspoon cinnamon
¼ teaspoon salt

2 eggs, beaten
½ cup melted shortening
1 cup zucchini, finely chopped
½ cup chopped walnuts
1 cup dried fruit, chopped

Preheat oven to 350°. Sift dry ingredients together. Mix eggs and shortening and mix with dry ingredients. Fold in zucchini, walnuts, and fruit. Bake for 55 minutes in lightly greased and floured loaf pan.

Pumpkin-Nut Bread

1 cup brown sugar, packed
⅓ cup shortening
2 eggs
1 cup canned pumpkin
¼ cup milk
2 cups flour
2 teaspoons baking powder

½ teaspoon salt
½ teaspoon ground ginger
¼ teaspoon baking soda
¼ teaspoon ground cloves
½ cup chopped walnuts
½ cup raisins

Preheat oven to 350°. Cream brown sugar and shortening together until light and fluffy. Add eggs, one at a time, beating well after each addition. Stir in pumpkin and milk. Sift together flour, baking powder, salt, ginger, soda, and cloves. Stir into pumpkin mixture. Beat 1 minute. Fold in nuts and raisins. Bake for 55 to 60 minutes in a lightly greased and floured loaf pan.

Applesauce Pancakes

3 tablespoons melted shortening or oil
2 eggs
3 tablespoons sugar
1 cup milk
⅔ cup applesauce

1½ cups sifted flour
2½ teaspoons baking powder
¼ teaspoon baking soda
¼ teaspoon salt
¼ teaspoon cinnamon

Mix shortening, eggs, and sugar. Alternately add milk, applesauce, and dry ingredients. Mix well. Bake on preheated griddle. Makes 12 to 18 pancakes.

BEVERAGES

Orange-Nog

2 cups orange juice
2 tablespoons honey

2 eggs
5 or 6 ice cubes

Put all ingredients into blender. Process on high speed until smooth. Makes 6 to 8 ½-cup servings.

Eggnog

2 eggs, separated
4 tablespoons sugar
½ teaspoon vanilla extract

2 cups milk
dash of ground nutmeg

Beat egg whites until stiff. Add sugar, egg yolks, vanilla and milk. Blend well and serve cold. Serve with a dash of nutmeg. Makes 4 ½-cup servings.

Cran-Orange Julius

1 6-ounce can frozen orange juice concentrate, thawed
1 cup milk
1 cup cranberry juice
1 teaspoon vanilla
10 to 12 ice cubes

In a blender mix orange juice, milk, cranberry juice, and vanilla on low speed. Add ice cubes and process on high speed until smooth. Makes 10 to 12 ½-cup servings.

Lemon-Orange Punch

1 12-ounce can frozen lemonade concentrate, thawed
1 6-ounce can frozen orange juice concentrate, thawed
4 2-liter bottles sparkling lemon-lime drink
ice cubes or fruited ice mold (page 96)

Mix all liquid ingredients in a large punch bowl. Add ice cubes or fruited ice mold. Makes 64 to 68 ½-cup servings.

Honey Apple Tea

6 tea bags
3 cups boiling water
⅓ cup honey

3 cups apple juice
lemon slices

In a 2-quart pot brew tea bags in boiling water. Remove tea bags, add honey and apple juice. Simmer till hot. Ladle into cups and garnish with lemon slices. Makes 6 to 8 teacup servings.

Cran-Apple Refresher

2 quarts cran-apple drink
1 6-ounce can frozen lemonade concentrate, thawed
1 quart club soda
ice cubes

In a large bowl or pot combine all ingredients. Makes 24 ½-cup servings.

Kiddie Kooler

1 pint lime or raspberry sherbet
1 12-ounce can frozen lemonade concentrate, thawed
4 cups water
1 quart lemon lime soda

Soften sherbet, and mix all ingredients together. Serves 8 to 10.

Spiced Tomato Juice

1 quart tomato juice
¼ teaspoon hot pepper sauce
4 teaspoons lemon juice
3 teaspoons Worcestershire sauce
½ teaspoon celery salt

Combine all ingredients. Chill and serve garnished with celery stalks. Makes 6 servings.

Cocoa Coffee

1 teaspoon hot cocoa mix
1 cup hot coffee
1 tablespoon whipped cream or ice cream

Add cocoa mix to coffee. Stir till dissolved. Garnish with whipped cream or ice cream. Makes 1 serving.

Hot Apple Cider

2 quarts apple cider or juice rind from 1 orange
1 teaspoon whole allspice 8 cinnamon sticks (optional)
1 teaspoon whole cloves

Combine all ingredients in a 3-quart pot, cover, and simmer 20 minutes. Strain and serve hot in cups or mugs. If desired, add a cinnamon stick to each serving. Serves 8.

Fruited Ice Mold

2 oranges, 2 lemons, and 2 limes, sliced
ice cubes

Place a layer of sliced oranges, lemons, and limes in a quart bowl. Top with a layer of ice cubes. Add another layer of fruit, then another layer of ice cubes. Fill with cold water to 1 inch of rim. Freeze at least 24 hours. Loosen by dipping mold in a pot or bowl of hot tap water.

COOKIES, DESSERTS, CANDY

Spritz Cookies

1 cup butter or margarine, softened
½ cup sugar
1 egg
1 teaspoon vanilla

2¼ cups flour
½ teaspoon baking powder
red and green food coloring
icing, nuts, sprinkles, etc. (optional)

Preheat oven to 375°. Cream butter or margarine; add sugar, egg, and vanilla. Beat until fluffy. Blend in flour and baking powder. Mix till well blended. To color cookies, divide dough and color with red and green food coloring as desired. Fill cookie press, form into shapes. Bake 8 to 10 minutes. Cookies may be decorated before baking, or when cookies are cool, they may be decorated with icing, then dipped into nuts, sprinkles, etc., or made into sandwich cookies. Makes 4 dozen cookies.

Danish Butter Cookies

3 sticks butter
1 cup sugar
2 egg yolks
2 teaspoons vanilla

¼ teaspoon salt, optional
4 cups sifted flour
1 teaspoon baking powder

Preheat oven to 375°. Cream butter with sugar. Add egg yolks, vanilla, and dry ingredients. Blend thoroughly by hand, or by mixer on low speed. Fill and use cookie press following directions that come with it. Force dough on ungreased baking sheet. If desired, decorate before baking. Bake about 8 to 10 minutes. Remove cookies carefully. They are very rich and break easily. Makes 6 to 8 dozen cookies.

Peanut Butter Wreaths

⅓ cup smooth peanut butter
⅓ cup butter or
   margarine, softened
⅔ cup light brown sugar

1 teaspoon vanilla
4 eggs
3 cups flour
2 teaspoons baking powder

Mix peanut butter and butter or margarine together. Add sugar and vanilla. Add eggs one at a time, then beat until fluffy. Sift flour and baking powder, add to creamed mixture, and mix thoroughly. Chill dough for ½ hour. Preheat oven to 375°. Roll about 1 tablespoon of dough between floured palms of hands to form a pencil-thick piece about 3 inches long. Form a circle, bringing one end over the other. Place on an ungreased cookie sheet. Bake for 8 to 10 minutes. Makes about 4 dozen cookies.

Variation:
        Peanut Butter and Jelly Cookies

Use crunchy peanut butter instead of smooth. Shape dough into balls. Place dough on pan. Press small indentation on each ball with thumb. Fill with jelly. Bake as above.

Gingerbread Cookies

½ cup butter or margarine
½ cup sugar
½ cup molasses
1 egg, beaten
3 cups flour

½ teaspoon baking soda
½ teaspoon ground ginger
½ teaspoon cinnamon
⅛ teaspoon white pepper

Preheat oven to 350°. In a large saucepan melt butter or margarine. Add sugar and molasses. Stir until sugar dissolves. Cool, then add egg and dry ingredients. Cover dough and chill. Divide into thirds, form a ball, and roll out on lightly floured surface to ⅛-inch thickness. Cut dough with floured cookie cutters. Place on greased cookie sheet, decorate with raisins, colored sugar, or cinnamon candies, or decorate with icing when cookies have baked and cooled. Bake for 10 to 15 minutes. Makes 12 to 16 cookies depending on size of cookie cutter.

Double Chocolate Chip Cookies

½ cup soft butter or margarine
6 tablespoons brown sugar
6 tablespoons granulated sugar
1 egg, well beaten
½ teaspoon vanilla extract
1 cup flour
2 tablespoons cocoa (unsweetened)
½ teaspoon baking soda
¼ teaspoon salt
½ cup nuts
1 6-ounce package chocolate chips

Preheat oven to 375°. Grease cookie sheets. Cream butter or margarine together with sugars. Add egg and vanilla. Mix well. Blend dry ingredients into mixture. Mix in nuts and chocolate chips. Drop by teaspoon on cookie sheet. Bake 12 to 15 minutes. Makes 3 dozen cookies.

Macaroons

1 14-ounce bag shredded flaked coconut
1 14-ounce can sweetened condensed milk
1 teaspoon vanilla
1 teaspoon almond extract
red and green candied cherries

Preheat oven to 350°. Grease baking sheets well. Mix together all ingredients. Drop from a teaspoon on baking sheet. Decorate with red and green candied cherries. Bake for 10 to 15 minutes until lightly browned. Using moistened spatula, remove immediately from baking sheet. Makes about 60 cookies.

LOVE FROM THE KITCHEN ~ 99

Cloud Cookies

1½ cups margarine or butter, at room temperature
1 cup brown sugar
1 cup sugar
2 eggs
2 teaspoons vanilla
3 cups flour
2 teaspoons cream of tartar
2 teaspoons baking soda
colored sugar (optional)

Preheat oven to 350°. Mix softened margarine or butter with sugars. Add eggs and vanilla. Beat well. Sift together flour, cream of tartar and baking soda. Add to batter. Blend well. Drop cookies from a teaspoon on ungreased baking sheets. Bake 8 minutes. Makes about 8 dozen cookies.

Note: these light, fluffy cookies can be decorated with colored sugar before baking.

Lacy Oat Cookies

⅔ cup light brown sugar
½ cup butter or margarine, softened
1 teaspoon vanilla
½ cup finely chopped nuts
1 cup oatmeal, uncooked
1 tablespoon milk
½ teaspoon baking powder

Preheat oven to 350°. Beat sugar and butter or margarine till fluffy. Stir in rest of ingredients. Drop from a teaspoon two inches apart on ungreased baking sheet. Bake 8 minutes. Let cookies stand for 3 minutes before removing with a wide spatula. Makes about 30 thin, lacy cookies.

Pecan Drop Cookies

1 cup butter or margarine, softened
½ cup sugar
1 egg
1 teaspoon almond extract

2¼ cups flour
⅛ teaspoon salt
½ teaspoon baking powder
1 cup chopped pecans

Preheat oven to 375°. Cream butter or margarine and sugar. Add egg and almond extract. Mix well. Stir in flour, salt, and baking powder, then pecans. Drop by teaspoon onto greased baking sheet. Bake 10 to 12 minutes until golden brown on bottom. Makes about 48 cookies.

Filbert Snow Balls

1 cup butter or margarine, at room temperature
½ teaspoon vanilla
⅓ cup sugar

⅔ cup ground filberts
1⅔ cups sifted flour
confectioner's sugar

Preheat oven to 325°. Mix butter or margarine, vanilla, sugar, and ground nuts. Add flour. Chill dough. Roll into small balls. Place on ungreased baking sheet. Bake until set, not brown. While still warm, dip carefully in confectioner's sugar. Makes 36 to 40 cookies.

Milk Chocolate Walnut Bars

½ cup brown sugar
½ cup butter or margarine, room temperature
1 egg
1½ cups flour
½ teaspoon baking powder
½ teaspoon vanilla
1 11½-ounce package milk chocolate chips
1 cup chopped walnuts

Preheat oven to 350°. Combine brown sugar, butter or margarine, and egg. Add flour, baking powder and vanilla. Press dough into 9 x 13-inch pan. Bake for 10 minutes. Remove from oven and immediately sprinkle with chocolate chips. Return to oven one minute. As soon as chips melt, spread evenly, then sprinkle nuts on top. Cool and slice. Makes about 4 dozen bars.

Raspberry Bars

Dough:
½ cup butter or margarine, softened
⅓ cup sugar
1 egg
1 teaspoon vanilla
1½ cups flour
½ teaspoon baking powder
12 ounces raspberry preserves

Topping:
¼ cup sugar
¾ cup flour
¼ cup margarine or butter, softened
½ cup finely chopped nuts

Preheat oven to 350°. Combine butter or margarine, sugar, egg and vanilla. Add flour and baking powder. Mix thoroughly. Press dough into a 9 x 13-inch pan. Spread dough with preserves. Mix topping of sugar, flour, margarine, and nuts together. Put this crumb mixture over the preserves. Bake for 20 to 25 minutes. Cool and slice. Makes about 4 dozen bars.

Date and Orange Bars

Filling:
2 cups pitted dates
½ cup sugar
¼ cup orange juice
1 teaspoon grated orange rind
½ cup finely chopped nuts

Combine all ingredients but nuts in saucepan. Cook over low heat stirring frequently until dates mash and filling is thick and creamy. Add nuts. Set aside.

Crust:
½ cup melted butter
   or margarine
¾ cup brown sugar
1 cup flour
½ teaspoon baking soda
1 cup oatmeal
confectioner's sugar
   for dusting top

Preheat oven to 350°. Blend butter and sugar. Sift flour and soda together and add to mixture. Add oatmeal and stir until well blended. Mixture will be crumbly. Pack ⅔ of mixture in a greased 8-inch square pan. Spread with date filling. Sprinkle remaining crumbs over top. Bake for 30 to 35 minutes. Dust with confectioner's sugar. Cool and cut into bars. Makes about 24 bars.

Holiday Honey-Fruit Bars

½ cup butter or margarine
½ cup brown sugar
½ cup honey
1 egg
1 teaspoon vanilla
1 cup flour
½ teaspoon baking soda
1 cup diced dried fruits
   (apricots, peaches, prunes,
   or dates)

Preheat oven to 350°. Grease 9 x 13-inch pan. In a large saucepan melt butter or margarine. Remove from heat and mix in sugar, honey, egg, and vanilla. Add flour and baking soda; mix till well blended. Mix in dried fruit. Pour into pan. Bake 25 minutes. Cool and slice. Makes about 48 bars.

Chewy Saucepan Brownies

½ cup butter or margarine
1 cup sugar
1 teaspoon vanilla
1 egg

⅔ cup flour
⅓ cup cocoa (unsweetened)
½ teaspoon baking powder
1 cup nuts, chopped

Preheat oven to 350°. Grease an 8x8-inch pan. Melt butter or margarine in a 2-quart saucepan over medium heat. Remove from heat. Stir in sugar and vanilla until blended. Beat in egg. Gradually add flour, cocoa, and baking powder. Stir until well blended. Add nuts. Spread batter in pan. Bake 30 minutes. Makes 16 2-inch brownies.

Saucepan Blondies

½ cup butter or margarine
1 cup dark brown sugar
1 teaspoon vanilla
1 egg*

1 cup flour
½ teaspoon baking powder
1 cup nuts

Preheat oven to 350°. Grease an 8x8-inch pan. Melt butter or margarine in a 2-quart saucepan over medium heat. Remove from heat. Stir in brown sugar and vanilla until blended. Beat in egg. Mix in flour and baking powder. Add nuts. Spread batter in pan. Bake 30 minutes. Makes 16 2-inch blondies.

*For a more cake-like blondie, use 2 eggs.

Variations:

Raisin Bars

Add ½ teaspoon cinnamon and substitute 1 cup raisins for the nuts.

Chocolate Marble Bars

While the batter is still warm, add ½ cup chocolate chips. When chips begin to melt, swirl through batter.

Chocolate Meringues

1 6-ounce package semi-sweet chocolate bits
4 egg whites
1 cup sugar
1 cup finely chopped nuts

Preheat oven to 350°. Grease cookie sheets. Melt chocolate in microwave or over hot water. Beat egg whites until stiff, then bear in sugar gradually. Fold in nuts and melted chocolate. Drop by teaspoonfuls two inches apart onto greased cookie sheets. Bake 10 to 15 minutes. Remove from sheets while still warm. Makes 4 dozen cookies.

Strawberry Coconut Meringues

¼ cup flaked coconut, very fine; additional for garnish
4 egg whites
1 teaspoon vinegar
1 teaspoon vanilla
1 cup sugar
½ cup uncooked oatmeal
strawberry ice cream
large package frozen strawberries, thawed

Preheat oven to 275°. Grease cookie sheet. Chop coconut till very fine and toast to a golden brown. Beat egg whites until foamy. Add vinegar and vanilla and beat until mixture forms soft peaks. Add sugar, slowly beating well as you add it. Beat mixture till it's stiff and glossy. Fold in oatmeal and coconut. On cookie sheet make 12 mounds and press a well in center of each. Bake about 45 minutes. Cool, and serve with strawberry ice cream topped with strawberries and more coconut. Serves 12.

Apple Crisp

5 cups peeled and sliced apples
1 cup uncooked oatmeal
½ cup brown sugar
½ cup melted butter or margarine
⅓ cup flour

Preheat oven to 375°. Put apples in an 8-inch square pan. Combine the rest of the ingredients, mixing until crumbly. Sprinkle on top of apples. Bake 30 to 45 minutes until apples are tender. Serves 6.

Plums and Pudding

1 cup butter or margarine, softened
1 cup light brown sugar
1½ cups flour
½ cup oatmeal
¼ teaspoon baking powder
1 16-ounce can purple plums, drained and pitted
1 egg, beaten
1 cup half-and-half
1 tablespoon white sugar

Preheat oven to 375°. Cream butter or margarine with sugar; add flour, oatmeal, and baking powder and mix until crumbly. Reserve ½ cup of crumb mixture and press the rest into a lightly greased 8-inch square pan. Put plums on crust, sprinkle with remaining crumbs, and bake for 15 minutes. Blend egg and half-and-half and white sugar. Pour mixture over plums and bake 20 to 25 minutes longer until custard is set. Cool and serve. Makes about 9 servings.

Frozen Lime Pie

1 6-ounce can limeade frozen concentrate, thawed
green food coloring
1 pint vanilla ice cream, softened
3½ cups whipped topping
1 prepared graham cracker crust
whipped topping and cherries to decorate

In a large mixing bowl beat concentrate and green coloring about 30 seconds. Slowly mix in ice cream till blended. Gently fold in whipped topping, mixing until smooth. Pour into pie crust and freeze until firm. Decorate with whipped topping and cherries. Serves 8.

Poppy Seed Slices

½ cup butter or margarine, room temperature
½ cup sugar
1 egg
½ teaspoon vanilla extract
¼ cup poppy seeds
1 cup flour

Cream butter or margarine and sugar. Mix in egg, then other ingredients. Refrigerate till dough can be handled. Shape into roll about 2 inches in diameter. Wrap roll in foil or plastic wrap and refrigerate 2 to 3 hours. Preheat oven to 325°. Cut roll into ¼-inch slices. Put cookies on ungreased cookie sheet and bake about 20 minutes. Makes 2½ to 3 dozen.

Mixed Nut Pralines

2 cups sugar
⅓ cup dark corn syrup
¼ teaspoon salt
⅔ cup evaporated milk
1 cup mixed nuts
½ teaspoon vanilla

Lightly butter a baking sheet. Mix sugar, syrup, salt, and milk in a heavy saucepan. Cook, stirring constantly over a medium heat until sugar is dissolved. Cook on medium heat without stirring until candy thermometer reaches 235° F (soft ball stage). Remove from heat, add nuts, and cool to lukewarm. Stir in vanilla then beat until mixture is thick and creamy. Drop from a teaspoon, forming patties. Do not disturb until patties are firm. Makes 1¼ pounds of candy.

White Raisin Clusters

6- to 7-ounce piece white chocolate
2 cups raisins

Butter baking pan. Melt chocolate in pan in the top of double boiler or in microwave container in microwave oven. Mix in raisins. Drop by teaspoonfuls onto waxed paper on cookie sheet. Chill until firm. Makes about 2½ dozen.

Variations:

Use milk chocolate or semi-sweet chocolate. Substitute coconut or peanuts for the raisins.

Honey Nuts

¼ cup honey
1½ cups sugar
½ cup water

½ teaspoon vanilla
5 cups unsalted nuts

Combine all the ingredients except the nuts in a saucepan. Cook, stirring frequently, until the sugar is dissolved. Continue cooking without stirring until syrup reaches 235° F on a candy thermometer, or soft ball stage. Add the nuts and stir until thick and creamy. Pour on waxed paper and separate nuts with a fork.

Uncooked Fondant

½ cup butter or margarine, softened
⅓ cup light corn syrup
¼ teaspoon salt
1 teaspoon vanilla or other desired flavoring
1 pound sifted confectioner's sugar
few drops food coloring (optional)

Combine butter or margarine with corn syrup, salt, and flavoring. Add confectioner's sugar. Mix until smooth and creamy. Knead in coloring. Refrigerate until firm. Shape as desired. Makes about 1⅓ pounds of candy.

Variations:

Mints

Flavor fondant with mint; tint with coloring as desired. Shape into patties. For chocolate mints, dip patties into melted chocolate and coat completely. Place on waxed paper. Refrigerate until firm.

Christmas Fondant

Shape fondant into balls. Trim with red and green candied cherries cut in half.

Fondant Stuffed Dates

1 recipe uncooked fondant (without food coloring)
few drops green food coloring
1¾ pounds pitted dates
nut pieces
sugar, granulated or confectioner's

Color fondant light green. Shape fondant into small rolls and stuff into pitted dates. Garnish with nuts and roll in sugar. Makes about 3 pounds of candy.

Double Peanut Brittle

1 cup sugar
⅛ teaspoon salt
1 cup white corn syrup
1 8-ounce package raw peanuts
1 teaspoon vanilla
1 tablespoon chunky
   peanut butter
1 teaspoon baking soda

Grease baking sheet. Combine sugar, salt, and corn syrup in a heavy saucepan. Cook over medium heat till syrup starts to boil. Add nuts. Continue cooking till syrup begins to turn golden brown. Remove from heat and stir in vanilla and peanut butter. Mix quickly and thoroughly. Mix in baking soda. Mixture will swell. Pour mixture onto baking sheet and cool. Break into pieces. Makes about 48 pieces.

English Toffee

1½ cups butter
2 cups sugar
2 tablespoons water

2 cups finely chopped almonds
½ teaspoon vanilla
1 6-ounce package semi-sweet chocolate chips

Grease baking sheet. Combine butter, sugar, and water in a heavy saucepan. Stir until mixture boils. Reduce heat to low, and continue stirring until candy thermometer reaches 300° F. Remove from heat; stir in almonds and vanilla. Quickly pour onto baking sheet and spread about ¼-inch thick. While still hot, top with chocolate chips. When chocolate melts, spread evenly over nut mixture. Cool until firm, then break into pieces. Makes about 48 pieces.

Fruit and Nut Balls

1 pound uncooked dried fruit
   (such as apricots, raisins, prunes), finely chopped
½ cup ground nuts
confectioner's sugar

Mix fruit and nuts together. Refrigerate several hours until firm. Shape into 1-inch balls. Roll in confectioner's sugar. Makes about 2 dozen balls.

PART 3
The Household Wrapped in Love

A clothespin doll made to resemble an angel,
A fluffy white dove floating free,
Ornaments crafted, and baked in an oven,
Then painted and hung on the tree,
A fragrant sachet to slide in a package,
Five puppets made out of one glove—
Trimming and gifts add more warmth to the season
When they're fashioned by hand . . . and with love!

CRAFTS

Gift Wrapping Ideas

Wrapping Paper: Use shelfing paper, brown wrapping paper, or white butcher paper. To marbleize, float a few drops of oil-based paint on water in a plastic container. Set paper on water. When you lift paper up, design of the paint will have adhered. Let paper dry before wrapping gift.

You can hand print with designs cut from sponges, potatoes, or linoleum block dipped into watered-down acrylic paint.

Decorations: Decorate boxed gifts to look like houses, clothing, and toys. Dried flowers, evergreen sprigs, colored paper, pieces of felt, and trimming can be glued on packages. Coffee cans and cookie tins can be painted and decorated with stencils, paints, and glue-ons.

Plastic garbage bags can be decorated with colored tape, self-adhesive label dots, and self-adhesive foil stars.

Jar Bonnets: Cut a circle of fabric 3 inches larger than diameter of jar lid. Trim edges with a pinking shear, or sew on lace or rick-rack edging. Attach circle to jar over lid with a rubber band. Cover rubber band with heavy yarn or with ribbon.

Baskets: Choose a basket with open weave and weave colorful ribbon through holes. Tie big bow on handle.

Salt-and-Flour Clay

4 cups flour
1 cup salt
1½ cups water

Put all ingredients in mixing bowl. Knead until smooth. Place dough in airtight container and remove pieces as needed.

Shaping the clay:
- Use only a small amount of clay at a time.
- For flat pieces, roll out clay on lightly floured surface to ⅛-inch to ¼-inch thickness. Cut out shapes with a cookie cutter or cut around paper pattern with a knife. Three-dimensional details such as buttons and bows can be added. To join pieces, moisten area where contact is to be made, and apply piece. Baking will cement the pieces together.
- Clay will dry best if it is under ½-inch thick.
- To hang as ornaments, insert a hanger into the top center. Hangers can be made from a loop of craft wire or a small

hairpin, or a paper clip can be straightened and cut into two hooks. For attaching hangers to ornament, a hole can be made with a cocktail straw or a toothpick. Make sure the hole is ¼ inch from the edge.

Finishing techniques:

- Set oven to 250°. Place shapes on ungreased cookie sheet.
- Bake 2½ hours or until completely dry. Remove from cookie sheet and cool.
- Using fine sandpaper or emery board, smooth any rough edges.
- Defining lines and details can be outlined in pencil.
- Paint the design using acrylic paints, watercolors, or poster paints, adding this year's date or personalizing the decoration if you wish. Be sure to paint the sides and back. Make sure one coat of paint is dry before you add the next color.
- For a finishing touch, spray with 2 or 3 coats of quick-drying varnish. Clear nail polish or clear shellac can also be used. Be sure to coat sides and back.

Pom Pom Decorations

Materials: Pom poms in assorted colors and sizes, felt tip permanent marker, paper, ribbon or lace, felt, feathers, small black beads, and wiggle eyes.

Bird: For a small bird, use a ½-inch pom pom for head and 1-inch pom pom for body. For a larger bird, use 1-inch pom pom for head and a 1½-inch pom pom for body. Glue together the two sizes. Cut a small triangle out of paper, fold in half, and glue on for beak. For a realistic bird, glue on small black beads for the eyes. Add feathers for wings and tail. For a cute-styled bird, add wiggle eyes and make wings and tail out of felt, ribbon, or

THE HOUSEHOLD WRAPPED IN LOVE ~ 115

construction paper. Construction paper and ribbon can be fringed and curled with a knife or scissors. Finish with small circle of felt glued to base of bird, or tie a thread to top to hang as ornament.

Christmas Elf: Glue 1-inch pom pom to 1½-inch pom pom for head and body. Glue on ½-inch pom poms for arms and legs. Glue on wiggle eyes, green felt ears and nose, and red felt mouth and bow. To make hat, form a half circle of felt into a cone, glue, and trim with white pipe cleaner and green felt trim.

Bunny: Glue ½-inch pom pom to 1-inch pom pom for head and body. Glue on ½-inch pom pom for tail. Make ears out of felt. With permanent marker, draw nose and mouth on thin paper and glue this onto head. Glue on wiggle eyes. Make paws out of felt or ¼-inch pom poms. Make base out of felt or tie a loop of thread to top to hang as ornament.

Snowman: Glue 1-inch pom pom to two 1½-inch pom poms. Add wiggle eyes. Make mouth and buttons out of felt or construction paper. Arms can be made out of tree or bush twigs or ¼-inch pom poms. Trim with felt or fabric scarf. Make base out of felt or tie a loop of thread to top to hang as ornament.

Stained-"Glass" Ornaments

Materials: Clear plastic (of at least the weight of food storage bags), aluminum foil, permanent markers, thin sheet of cardboard, tape, glue.

General directions: Choose design. Cut cardboard to desired shape and size. Cut plastic to cover cardboard, adding ½ inch to all edges. Lay plastic over design you wish to copy. Copy all lines on plastic with dark thin-line permanent marker. Color in spaces as desired with markers of various colors. Wrinkle a piece of aluminum foil. Cover cardboard with foil, lapping it over to the back. Lay colored plastic over foil and tape to the back of the cardboard. Glue wire or string loops to the back of ornament. Cut a piece of foil to shape of ornament and glue to back to finish. Or the ornament can be framed in a mini-needlecraft frame.

Stained-"Glass" pictures: To enlarge pattern, copy design on tracing paper. Rule paper into ¼-inch squares. On a larger sheet of paper, rule 1-inch squares. Copy line for line onto larger paper. A 4x5-inch design will become a 16x20-inch design. Proceed with general directions. When design is finished, there is no need to back with more foil; design may be framed instead.

Stained-"Glass" containers. Choose a clear plastic container. Tape design pattern to the inside of container. When design is finished, line container with wrinkled aluminum foil and fill with a treat or crushed paper so foil retains shape.

Foil Gift-Wrap Decorations

Materials: Foil gift-wrap, scissors, stapler, invisible transparent tape, and trimmings such as ribbon, sequins, and lace.

Fan: Cut piece of foil gift-wrap 2½x12-inches. Fold into accordion pleats ½-inch wide. Staple or wrap tape around base of fan. Spread fan and decorate with glued-on trim. Attach a loop of thread to the top for a hanger.

Pleated Circle: Make a fan as above but use 24 inches of foil gift-wrap. Staple base and trim paper very close to staple. Spread into a circle and glue or tape together. Trim as desired, making sure center is covered. Attach a loop of thread for a hanger.

Pleated Bow: Cut a 4-inch square of foil gift-wrap. Make a diagonal fold through the center and continue folding in ½-inch wide accordion pleats. Staple the center and spread the bow. Attach a loop of thread to the middle of the bow for a hanger.

Clothespin Dolls

Materials: Round-headed (wooden) clothespins, pipe cleaners, paint, marking pens, fabric, trimmings such as lace, ribbon, braid, etc., pom poms.

General directions: Position clothespin so a leg is on either side. To form arms, center a 4½-inch pipe cleaner 1 inch down from the neckline. Tape arms in place. Bend arms down over tape. Form hands by bending back pipe cleaner at its ends. If desired, paint doll and arms a matching color. Draw on face with paint or permanent markers. Dress doll by sewing, gluing, or wrapping fabric. Add hair out of pom pom, yarn, or loopy chenille.

Santa's Helper: Paint legs red or green. Make a 4-inch poncho out of felt; cut hole in center. Make belt with ribbon, pipe cleaner, or felt. Make a cone-shaped hat by rolling a half circle of paper or fabric. For ornament, attach loop of thread to hat for hanger.

Ballet Dancer: Cover chest with 1-inch ribbon. Make a 2-inch tutu ruffle out of lace or net and sew or glue in place. Tie a ribbon around waist, add pom pom for hair, and paint ballet slippers on tips of legs. For ornament, attach hanging loop.

Angel: Make an 8-inch circle out of fabric. Cut hole in center for head and slits 1 inch from neckline for armholes. Pull arms through and tie on a belt to gather fabric. Fasten wings out of felt, paper, or feathers. Glue halo out of wire or gold pipe cleaner to back of head. To hang as ornament, add loops to wings or head.

Foil Pan Ornaments

Materials: Foil pans (plain or textured), ball-point pen, permanent markers, glass stain (a transparent acrylic paint), trimmings, thin wire or string for hangers, old scissors, needle.

General directions: Cut rim off pan. Lay paper pattern on foil. Go over design with ball-point pen using pressure so lines will show through on foil. Cut out shapes with old scissors. Using permanent markers or glass stain, color and decorate ornament. Make hole for hanger with needle, string wire or cord through hole for hanger. (Note: Use rims from pans for small shapes such as icicles and diamonds.)

Butterfly: Proceed with general directions. Before hanging, bend wings on either side of butterfly body.

Caroler: Proceed with general directions. Bend arms forward before hanging.

Finger Puppets

Materials: Gloves, fabric, felt, yarn, wiggle eyes, marking pens, acrylic paint, thin ribbon, and needle and thread.

General directions: Cut fingers off of glove. Overcast finger edges if material ravels. Puppet base can also be made from felt or double knit fabric by sewing two finger-shaped pieces together. Choose design and finish with trimmings and paint or markers.

Tissue Paper Poinsettias

Materials: White, red, pink, and green tissue paper; invisible transparent tape; gold metallic pipe cleaners cut into 3-inch lengths; wire stems and floral tape (optional).

General directions: To make petals, cut tissue paper to form rectangle about 5x25 inches. Fold rectangle in half so that its length is 12½ inches, then halve it again, and yet again. In paper doll fashion, cut the folded tissue into a wedge shape (see illustration), rounded as shown. Leave a ½-inch margin beyond the tip of the wedge and at its base; unfurl. To make leaves, repeat above procedure using green tissue. Grasp 2 or 3 pipe cleaners as a core and gather the wedges by their ½-inch margin. Continue gathering and rolling the strip around pipe cleaners until several rows of petals form. Secure petals with tape at the base. Gather and roll leaf wedges around petals and secure with tape. Make a small hook at top of each pipe cleaner and straighten petals and leaves. (Cut properly, one 5x25-inch strip of tissue will make 2 flowers.)

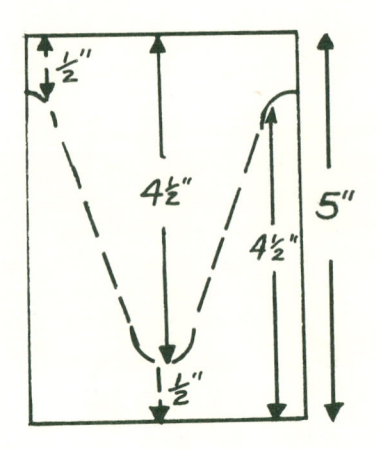

Package Decoration: Add ribbon to base of poinsettia and tape or glue to package.

Flower Arrangement: Tape poinsettias to a wire stem with green floral tape and arrange by inserting into plastic foam base in vase.

Wreath: Cover a wreath frame with green tissue strips wrapped diagonally around frame. Arrange poinsettias on wreath and glue in place.

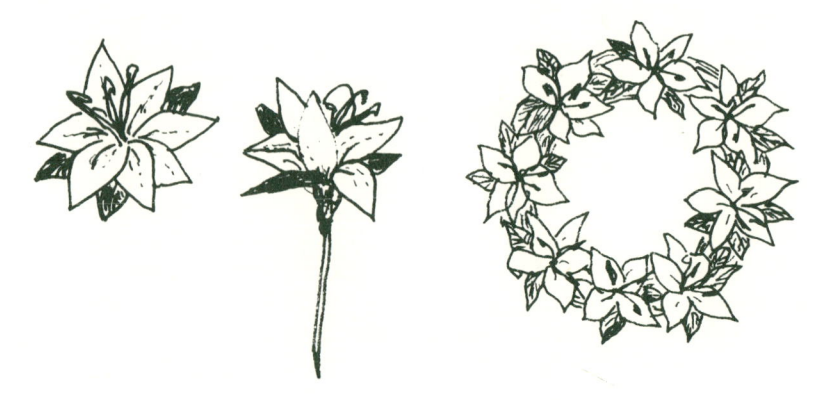

Sachets

Materials: 4½-inch-wide lace or eyelet, ribbon, trimmings, potpourri, needle and thread.

Instructions: Cut fabric into 3½-inch pieces. With right sides of fabric together, sew ¼ inch from edges on bottom and sides. Turn right side out. Leave top open, fill with potpourri, tie sachet closed with ribbon, and trim as desired. To use as ornament, add loop out of cord or wire for hanger.

Stuffed Felt Ornaments

Materials: Various pieces of felt, trimmings such as ribbons, sequins, beads, or braid, fiberfill or stuffing material of your choice, cord.

Instructions: Make a paper pattern of design. Cut out two pieces of felt using this pattern as a guide. Glue trimmings to front side of ornament. If desired, animal manes and tails can be stitched to wrong side of front fabric. Pin back of ornament to front, wrong sides together. Leaving a small opening at top for loop and stuffing, sew close to edge. Stuff ornament. Stitch on loop for hanging and stitch opening closed.

Patterns

These versatile patterns can be used for your gingerbread cookies, salt-and-flour clay ornaments, stained-glass ornaments, foil pan ornaments, or stuffed felt ornaments. You can change the trimmings to your liking and create your own special look, and the patterns can be enlarged as noted on page 117.

NOEL

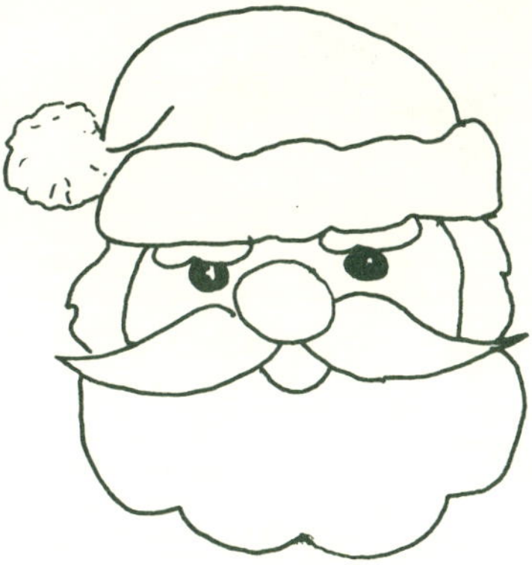

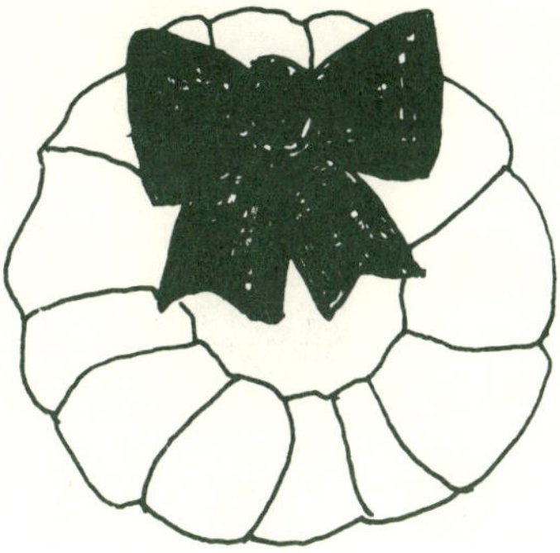

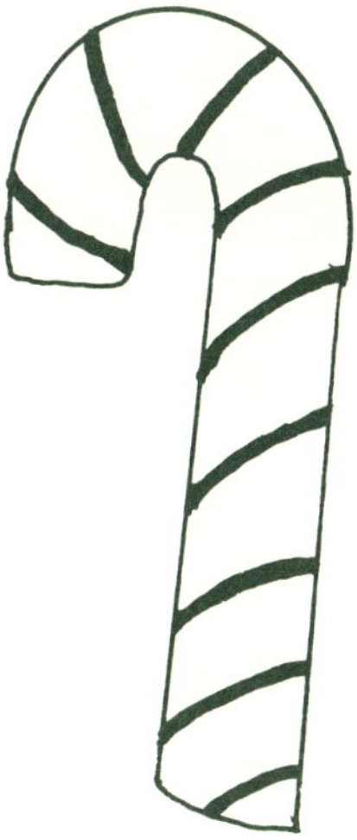

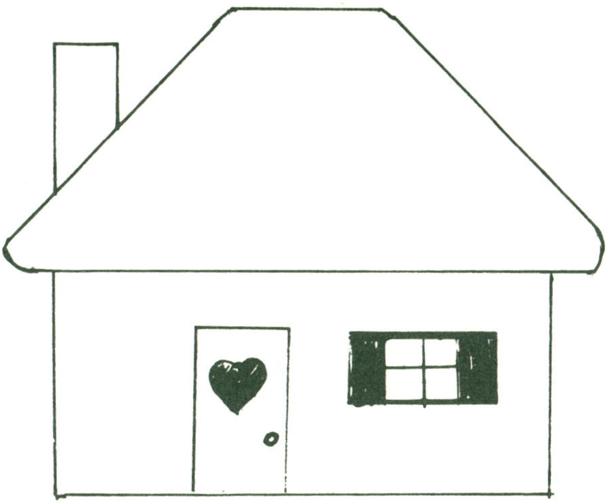

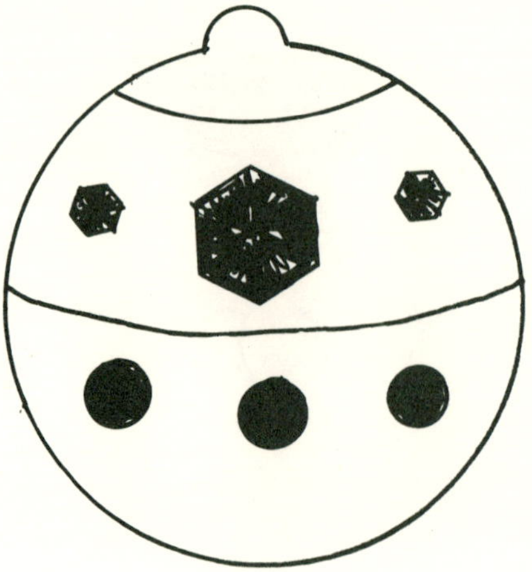

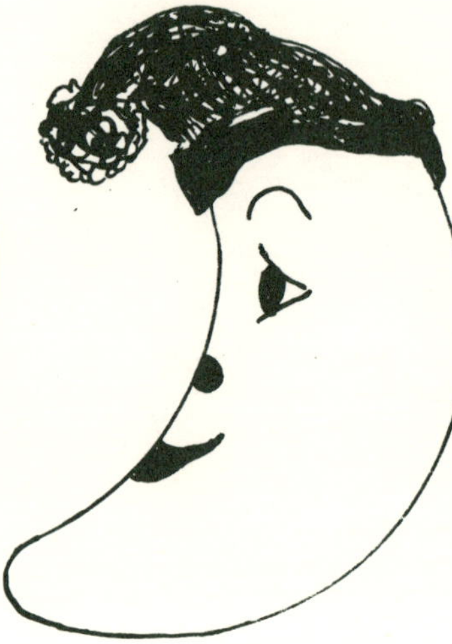

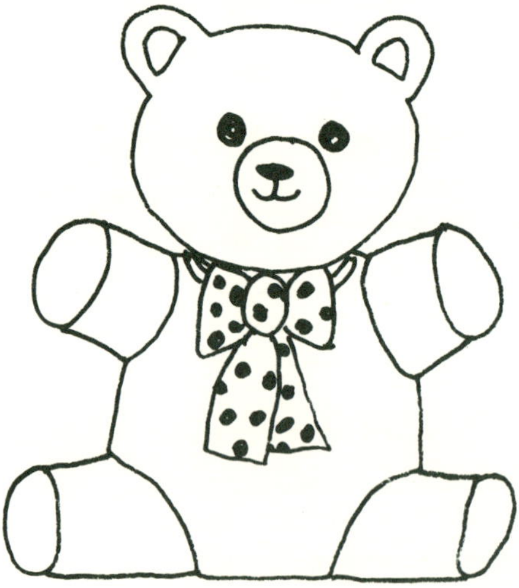

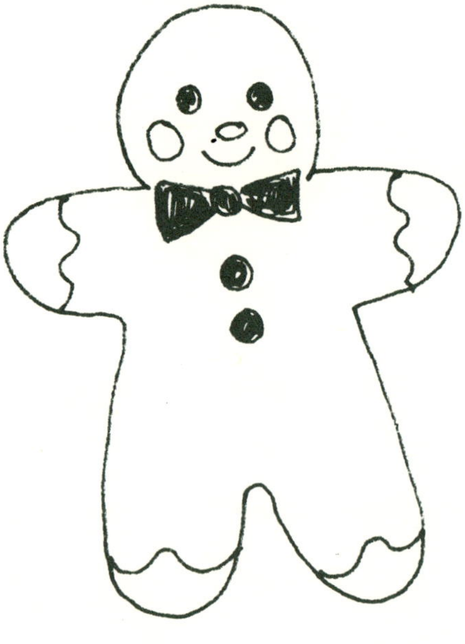